THE CLASSIC CAMERA

Street and Landscape

The Classic Camera

Street and Landscape

Wolf Arnold

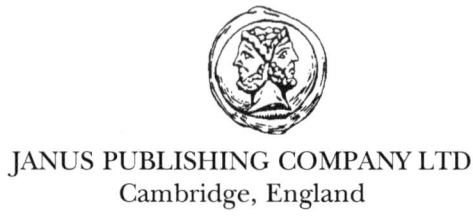

JANUS PUBLISHING COMPANY LTD
Cambridge, England

First published in Great Britain 2017
by Janus Publishing Company Ltd
The Studio High Green
Great Shelford
Cambridge CB22 5EG

www.januspublishing.co.uk

British Library Cataloguing-in-Publication Data
A catalogue record for this book is available from the British Library

ISBN 978-1-85756-868-4

Cover Design: Janus Publishing Company Ltd

Front cover image: Scaliger Castle, Verona, Italy
Back cover image: Stadtschloss in Darmstadt, Germany
Both images were supplied by the author

If any person recognises themselves in a photograph, I apologise for using this image without their permission.

Printed and bound in Great Britain

Introduction

The term 'classic' evokes certain passions for objects that once were, and still are today, admired with enthusiasm for their style, craftsmanship and durability, not to mention a nostalgia for things of the past. There are classic cars, classic trains, classic watches and classic cameras. The latter work with film, not a digital memory card. They are easy to operate and obviously more fun. No 'menus', no fancy features, just mechanical dials, manual focus, frame your subject and shoot. I recall seeing an ad in a magazine, though it was not a photography magazine, for a Leica camera, a Leica M 6. The text extolled the fine craftsmanship with which every Leica is put together, and I remember reading that 'it was made with love and care and there seems to be a soul in every Leica. Try to find this in one of those digital cameras.'

This book is an extension to my previous work, *The Analog Camera*. They do not pretend to be books on outstanding photography, but rather a mirror of everyday situations, of everyday people in their everyday environment. Naturally, I could not resist the temptation to include landscapes and historical landmarks.

W. A. 2017

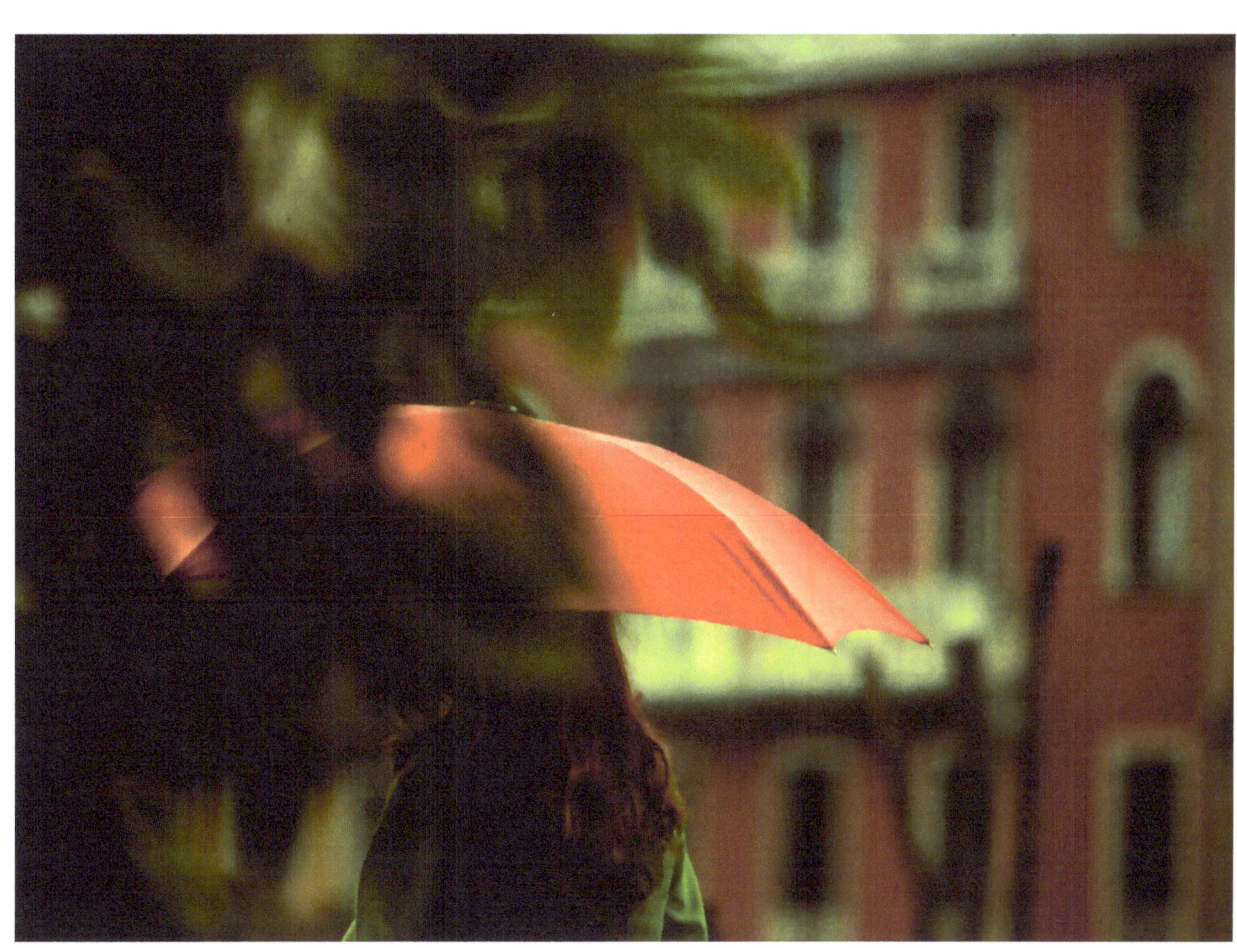

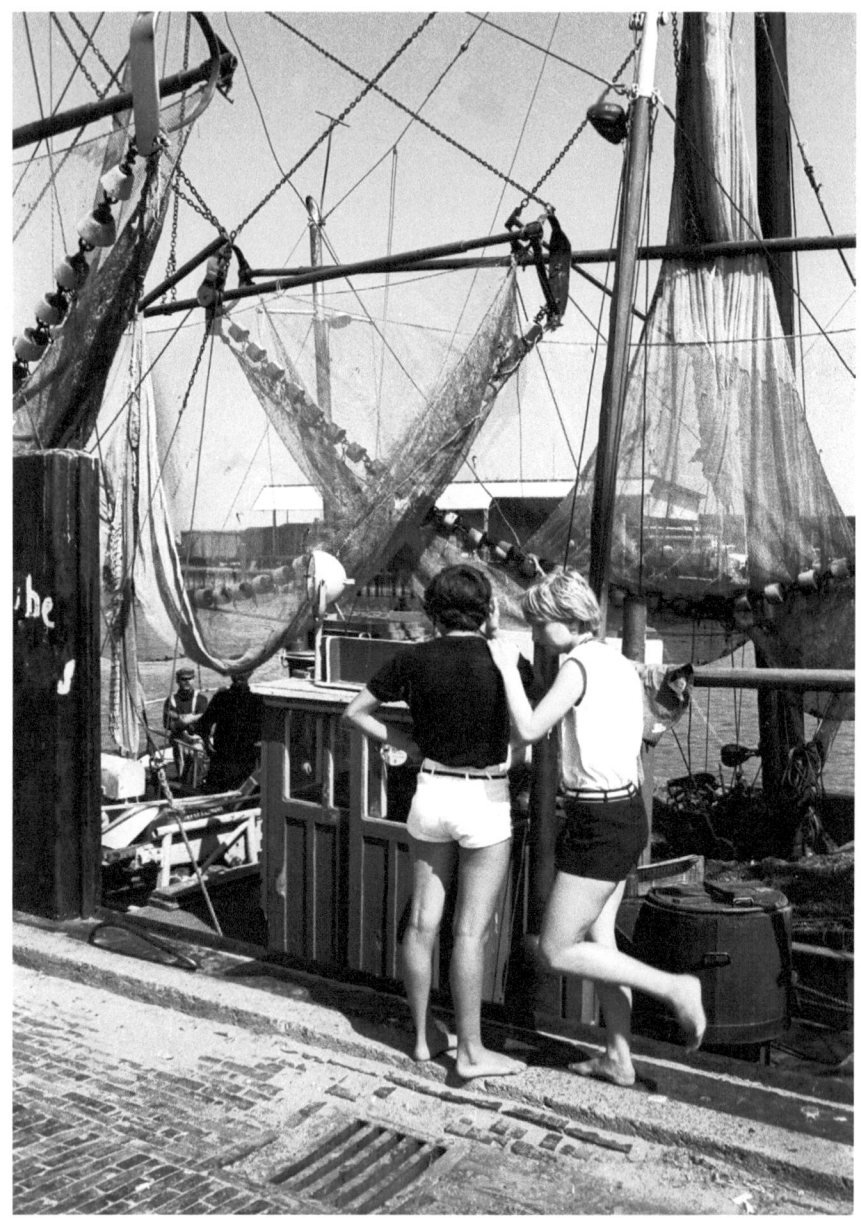

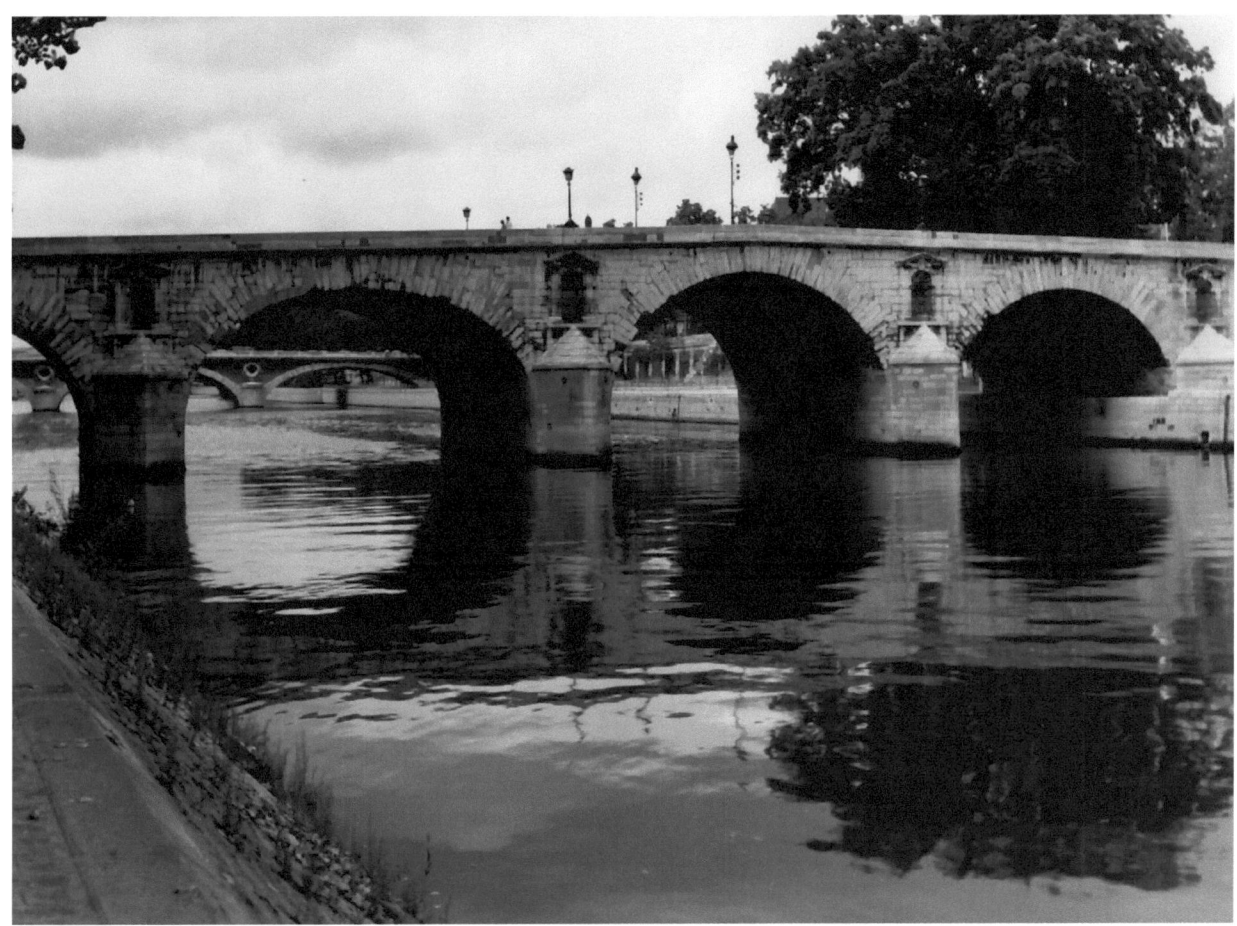

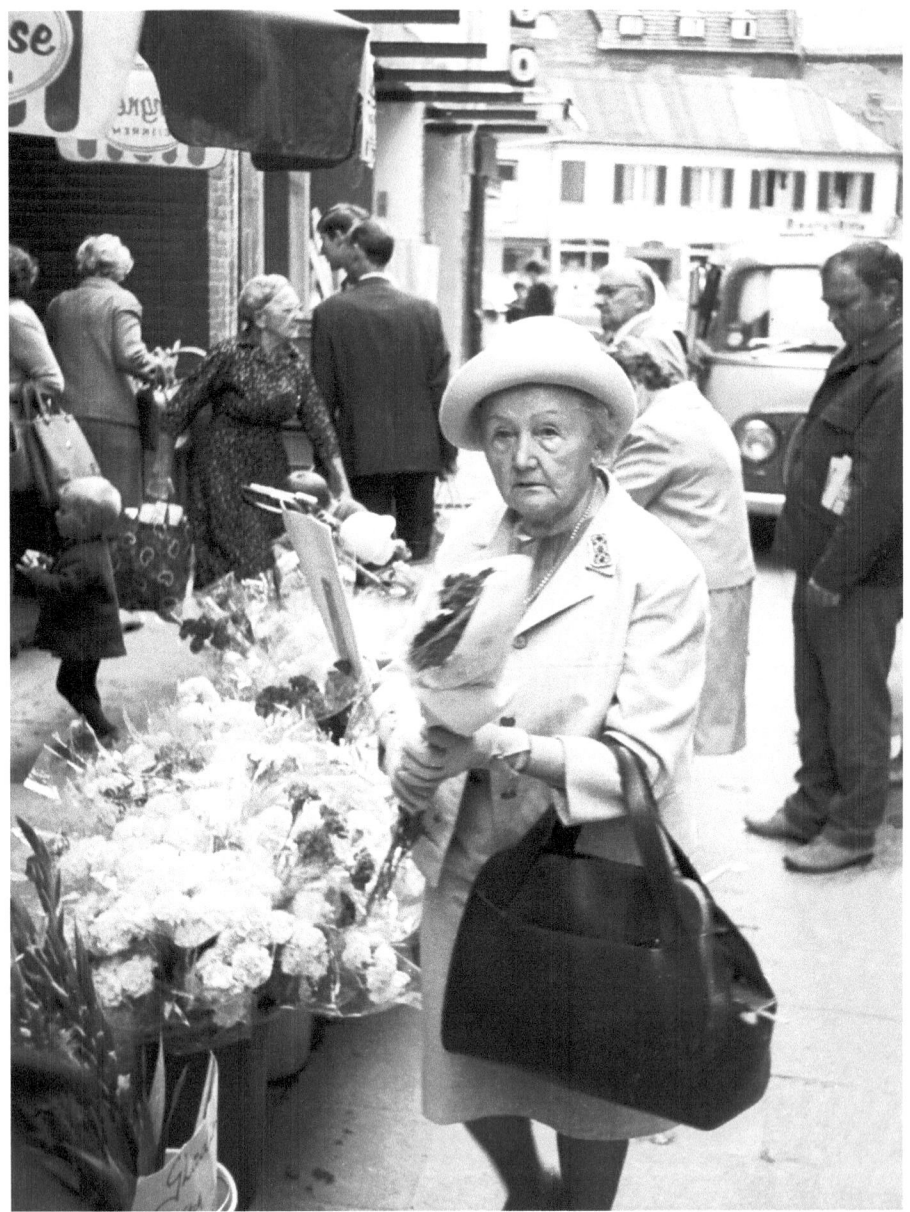

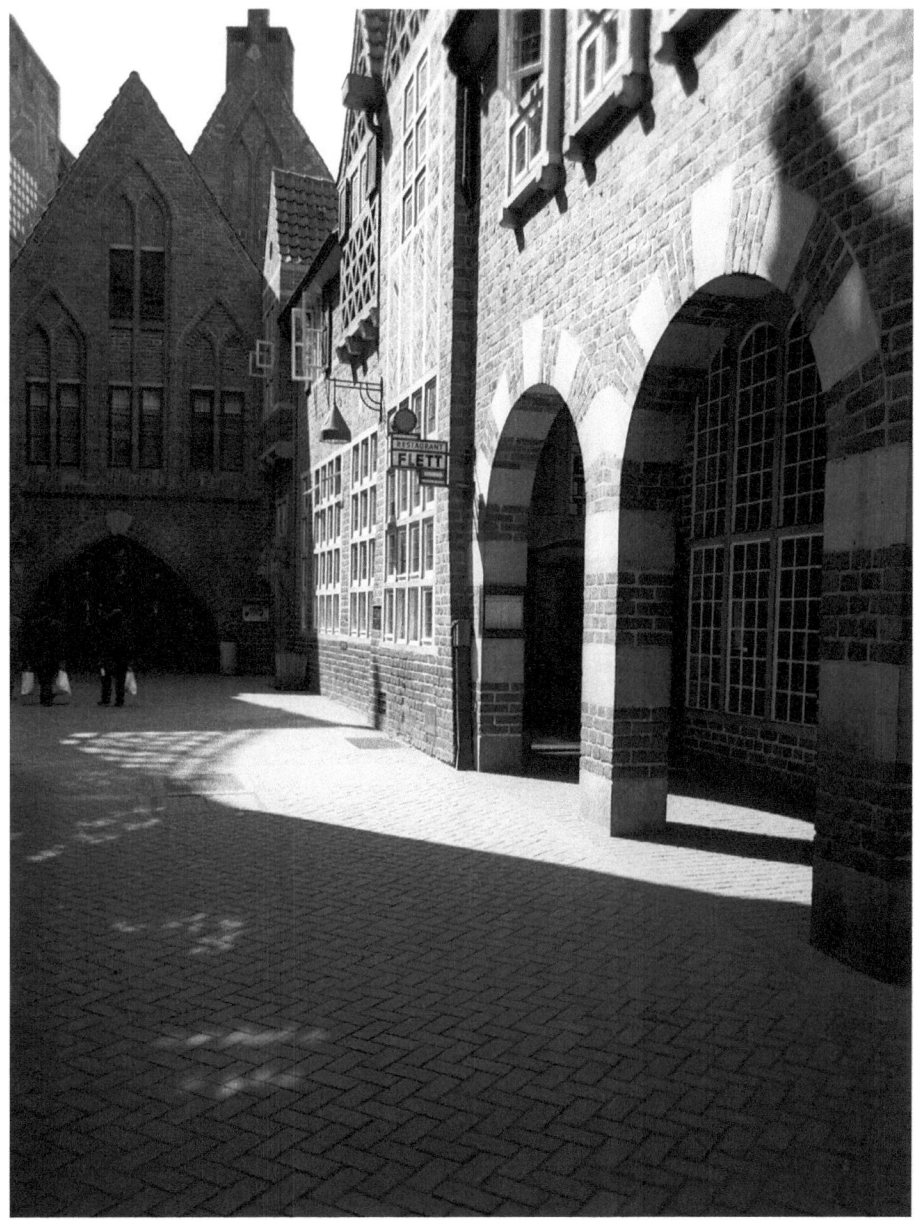

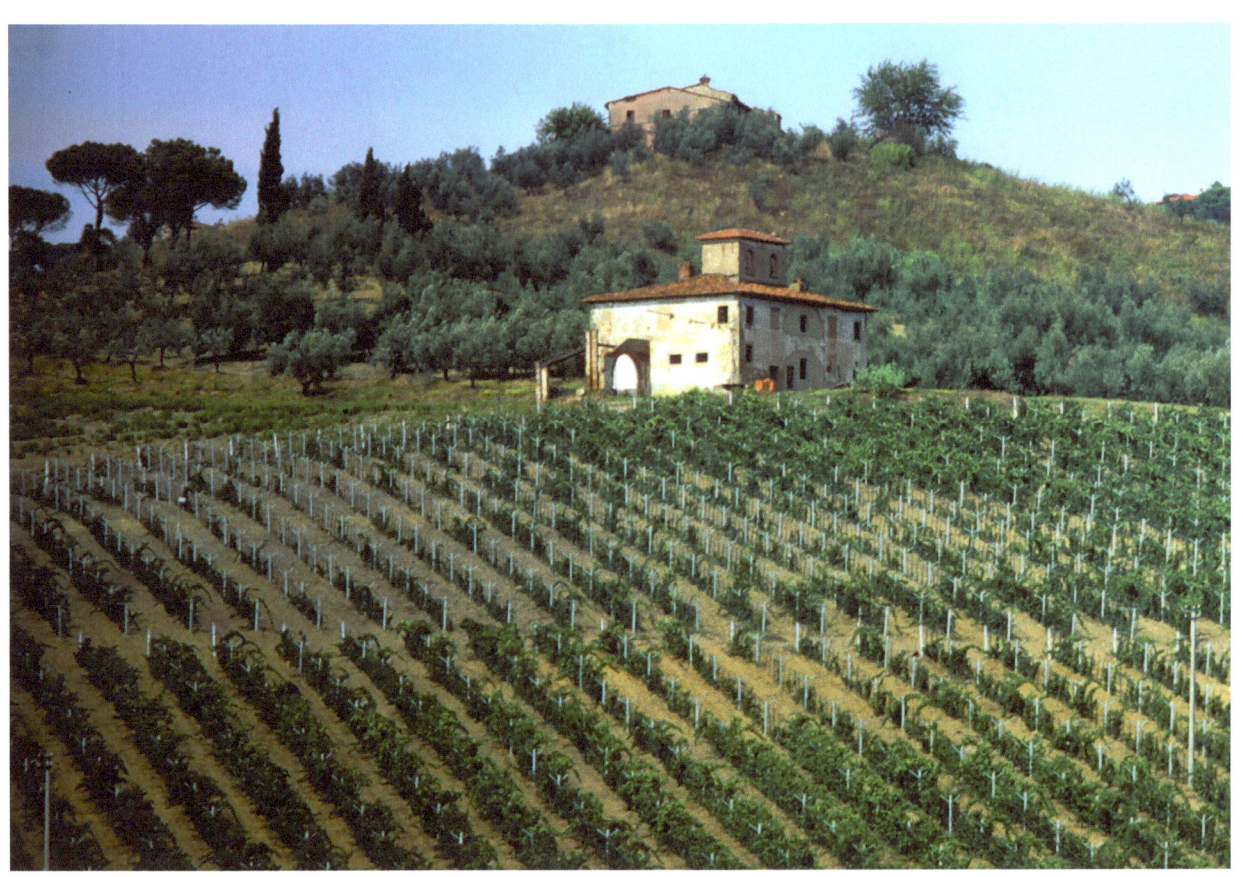

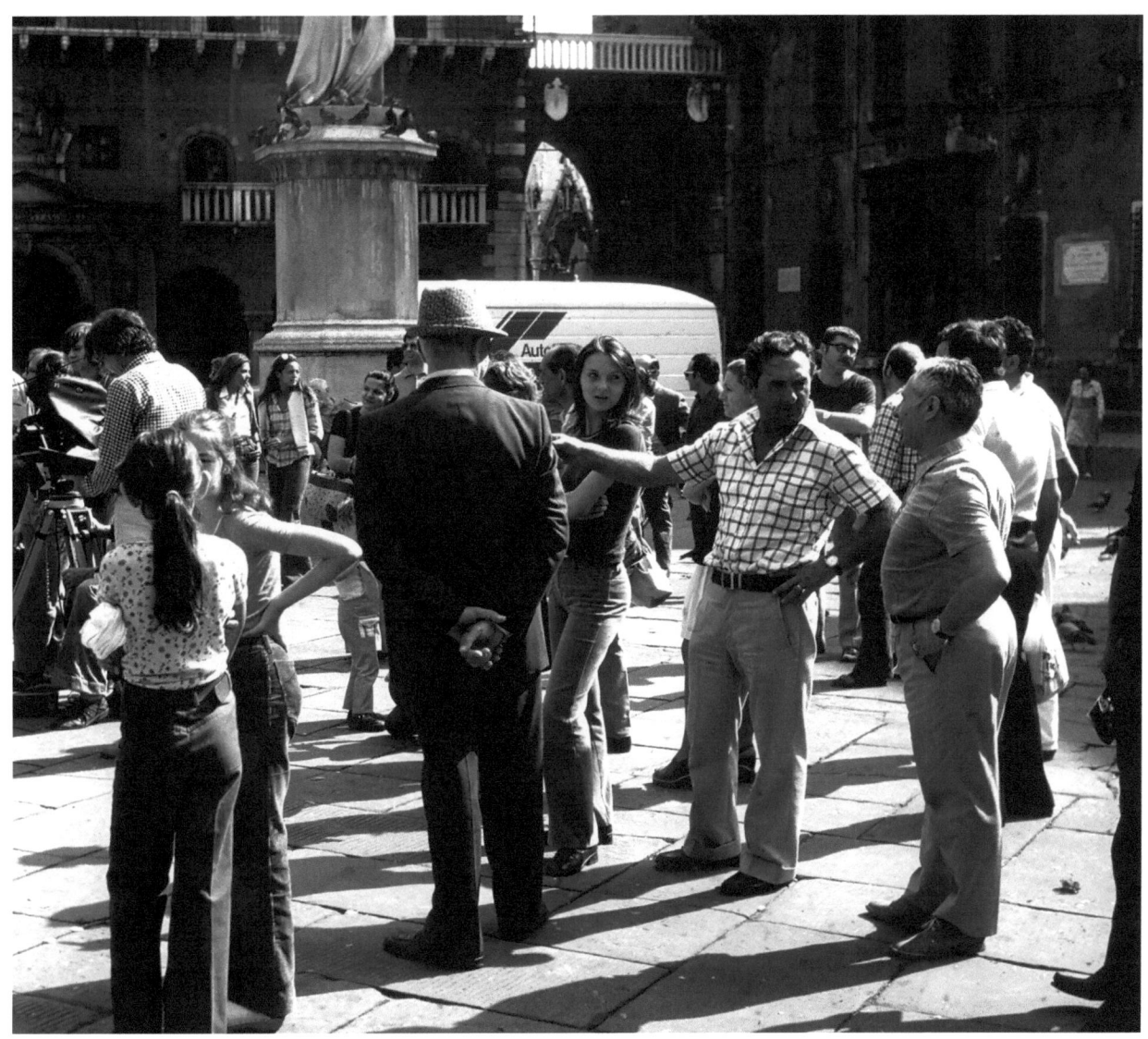

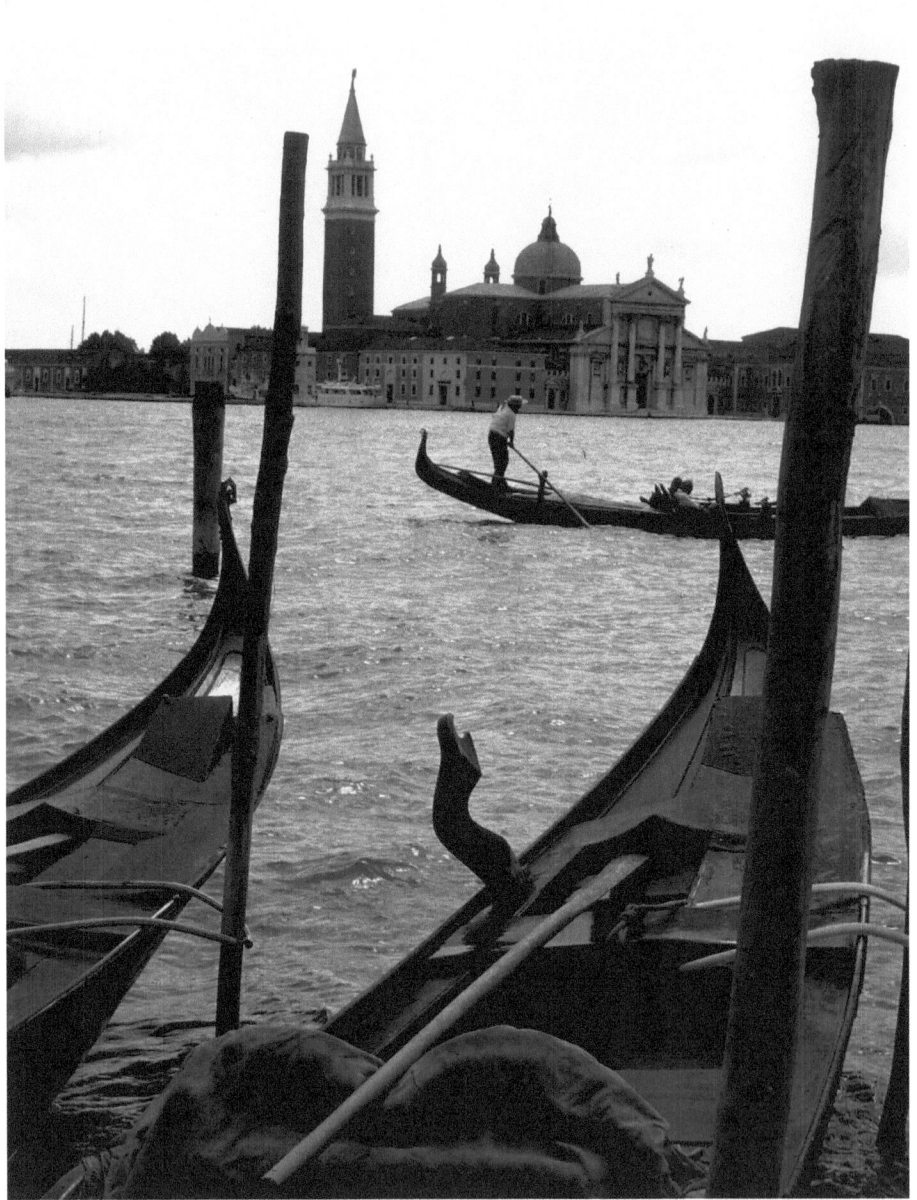

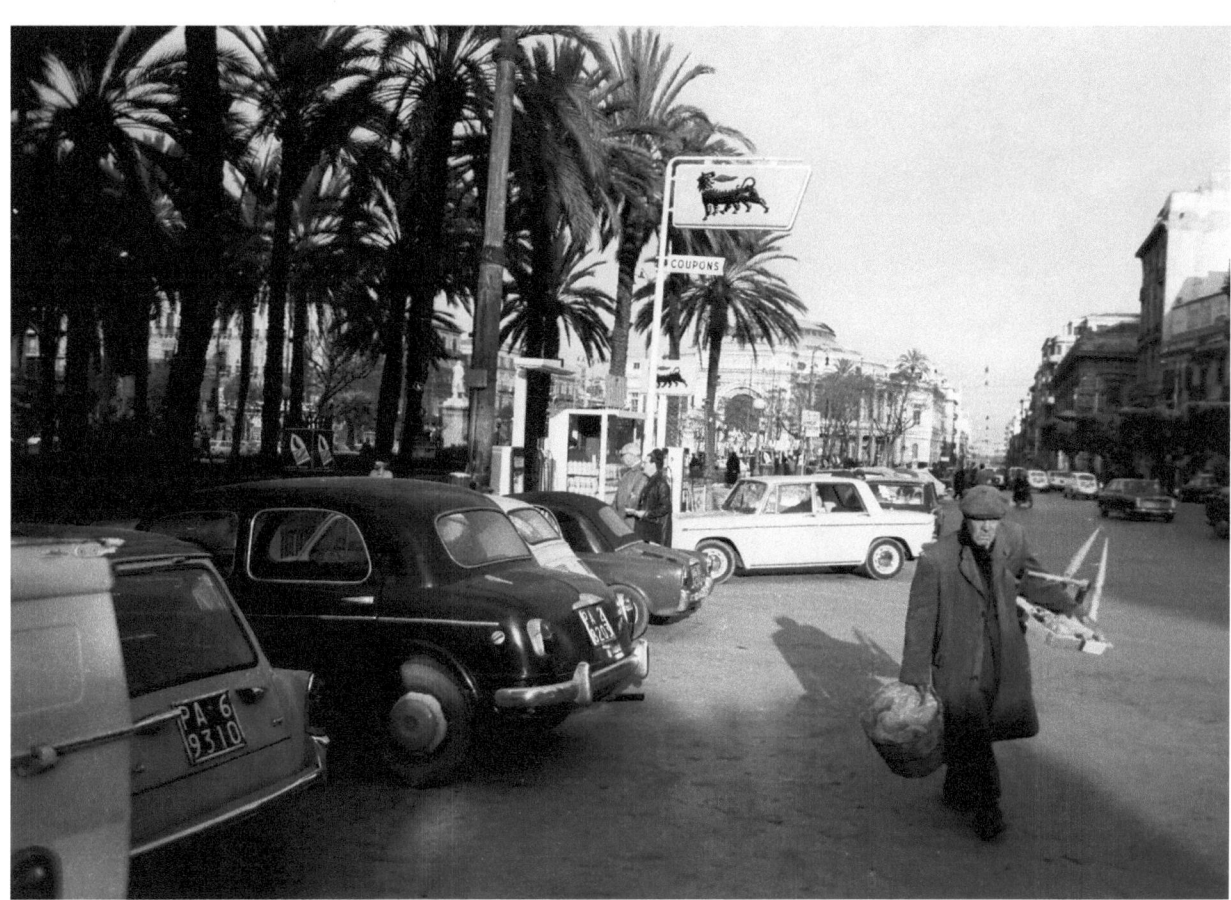

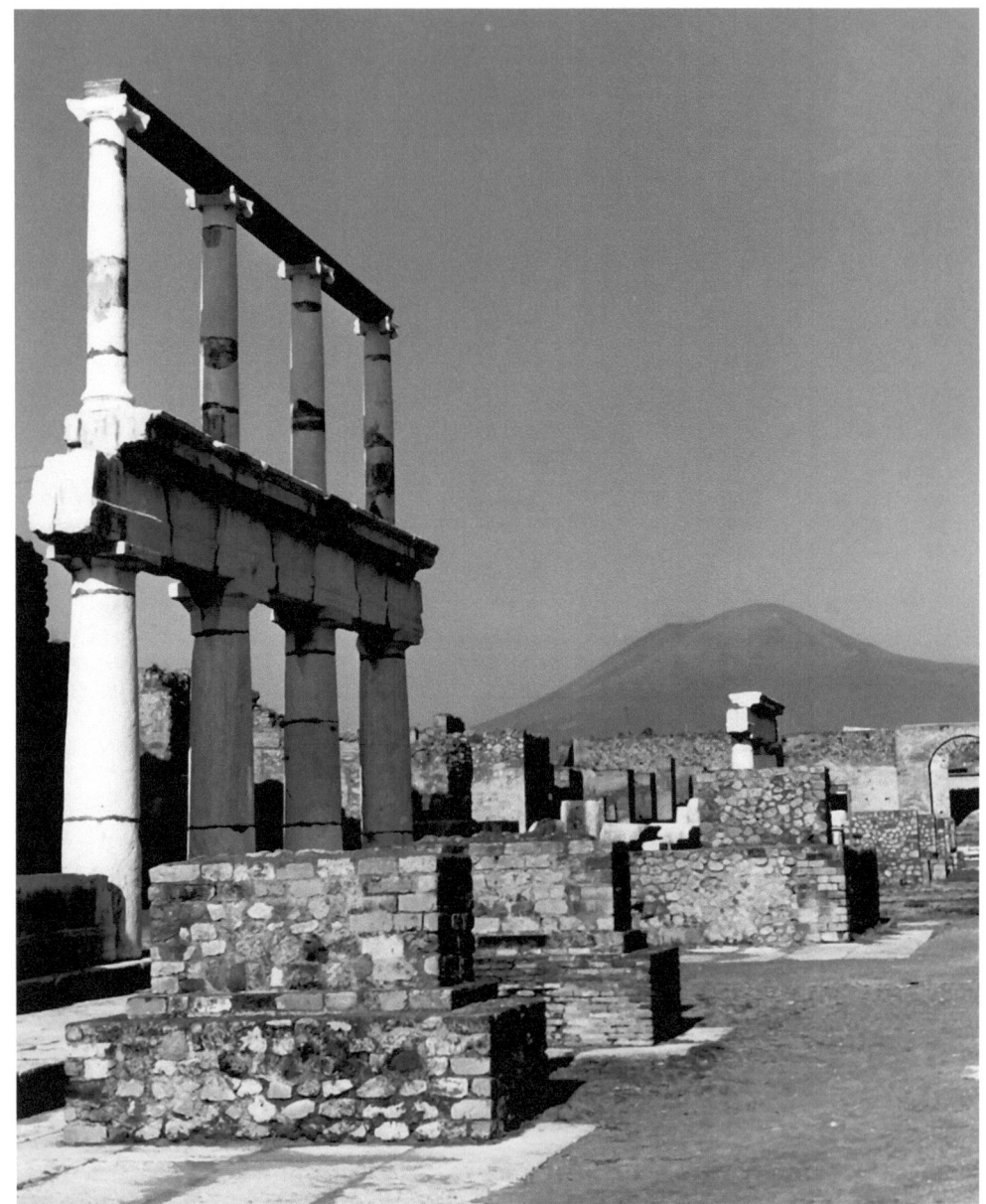

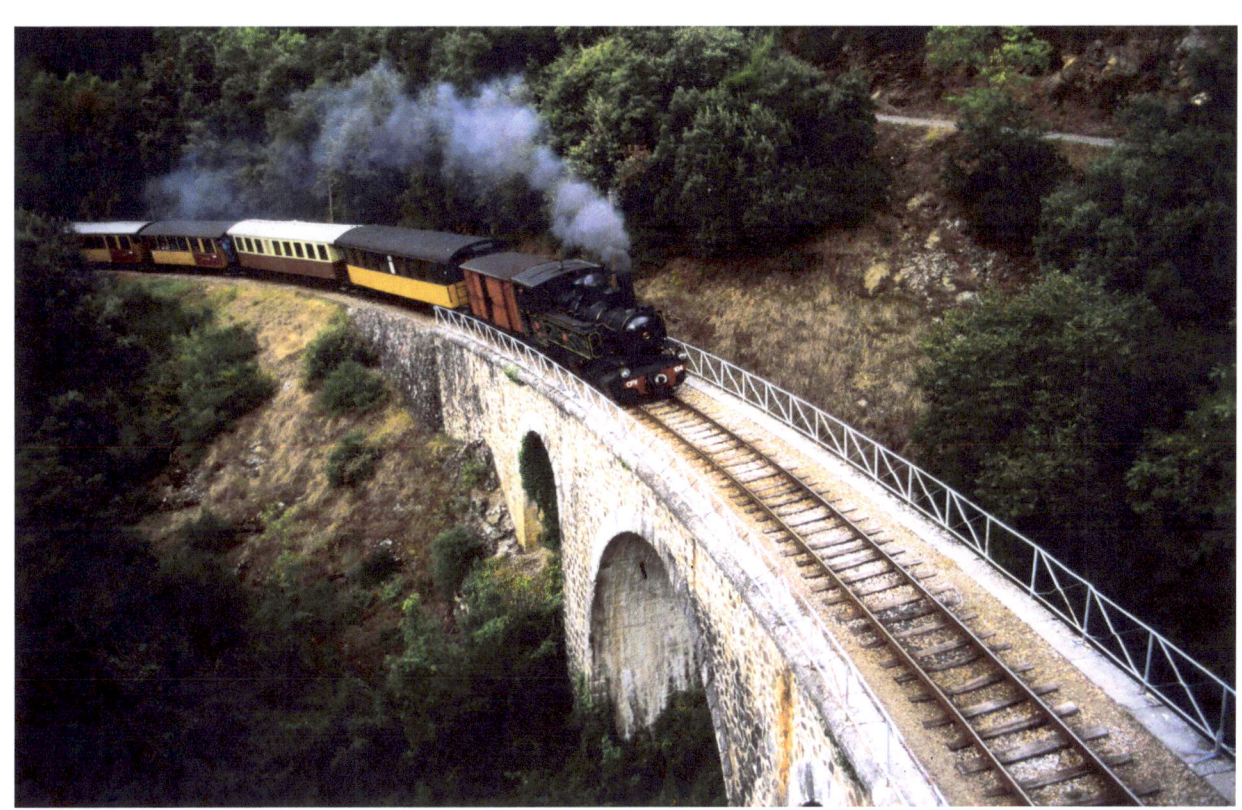

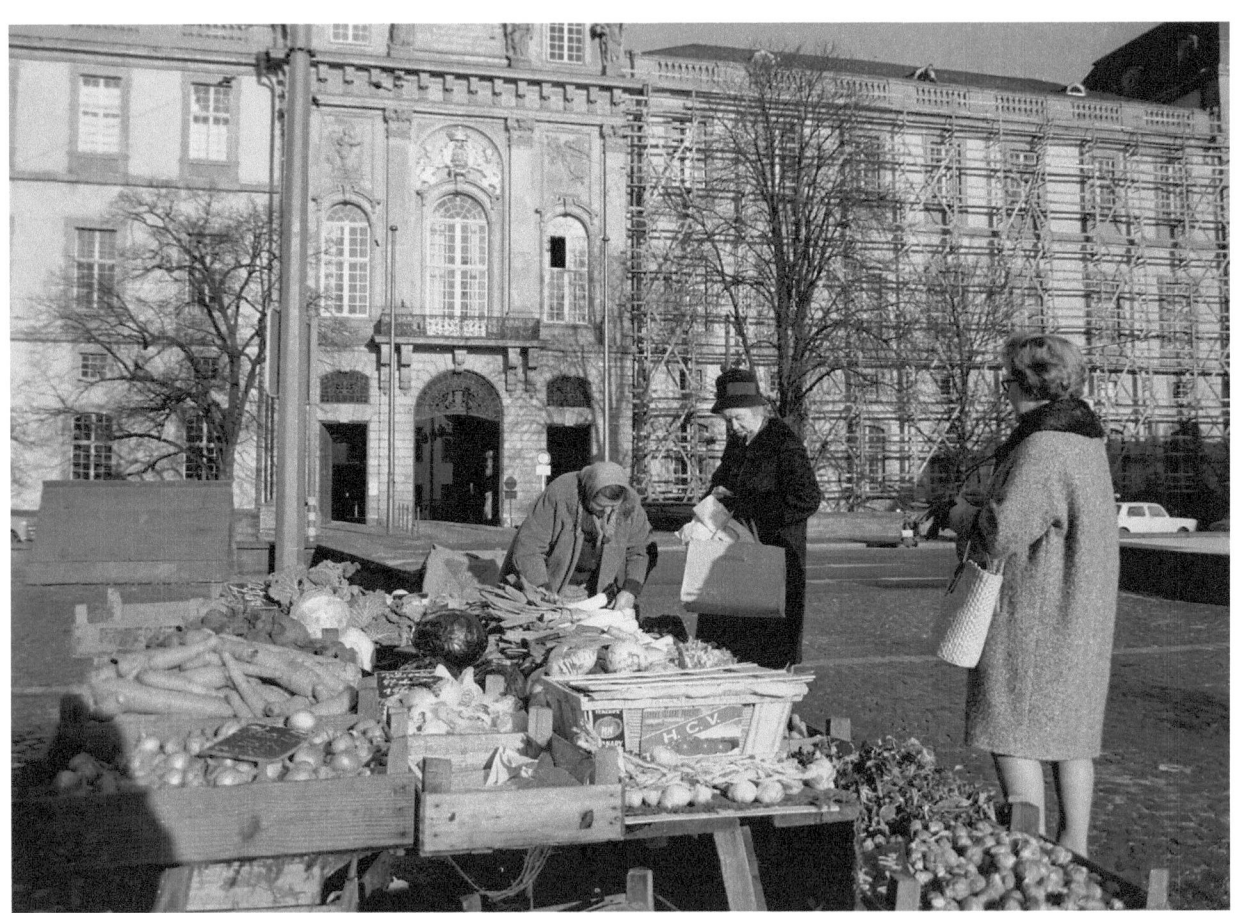

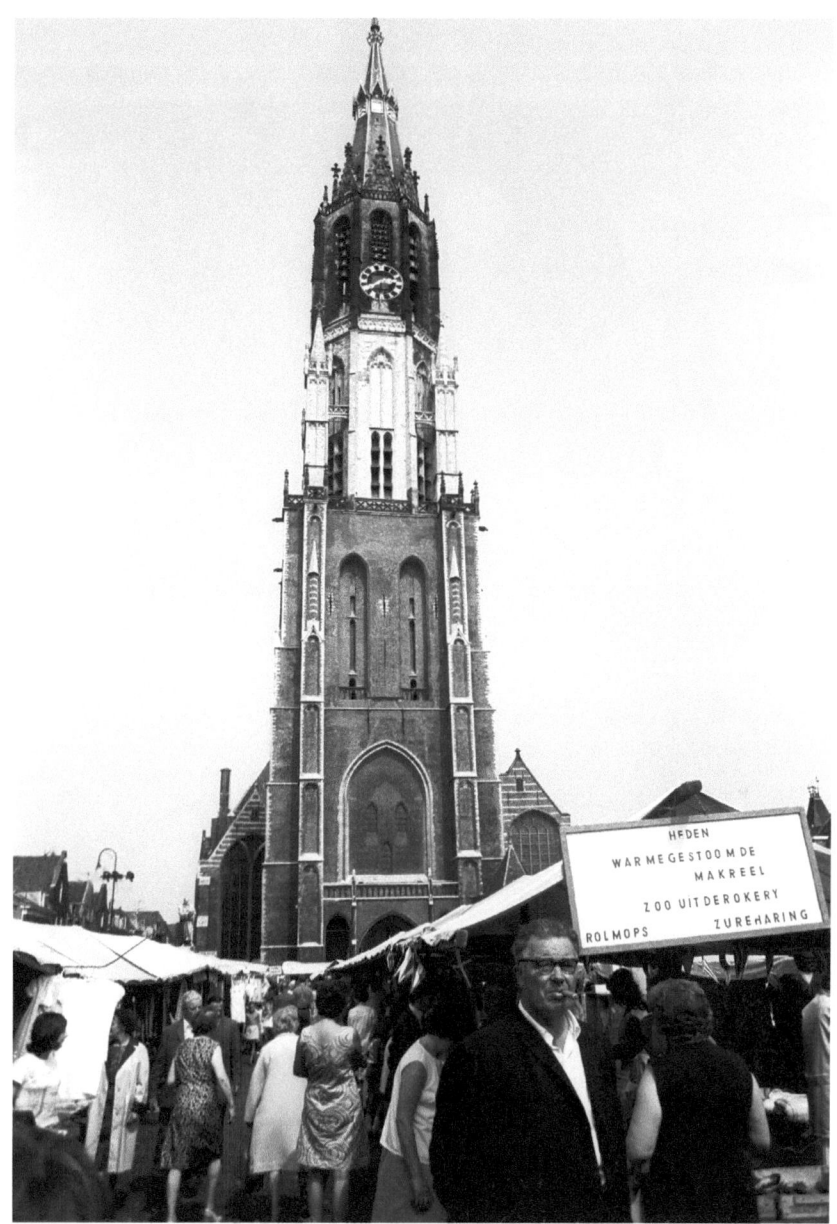

13

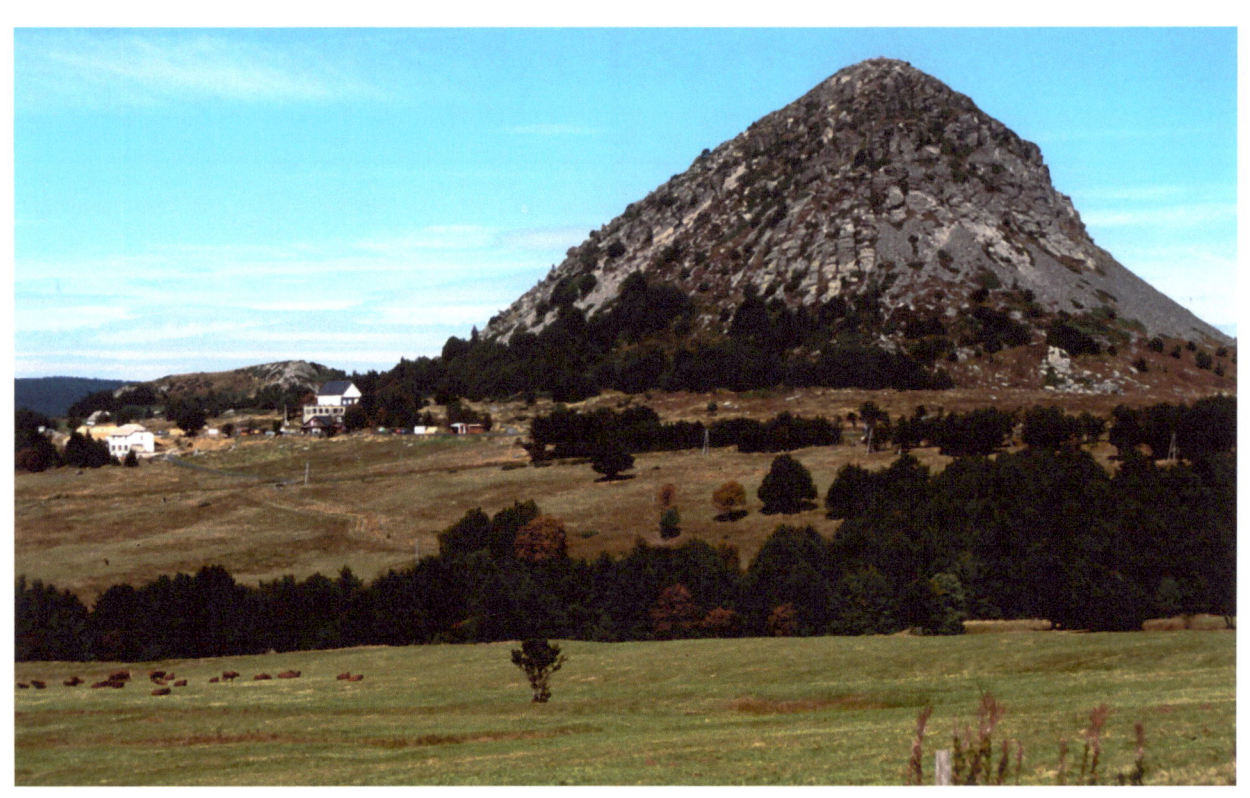

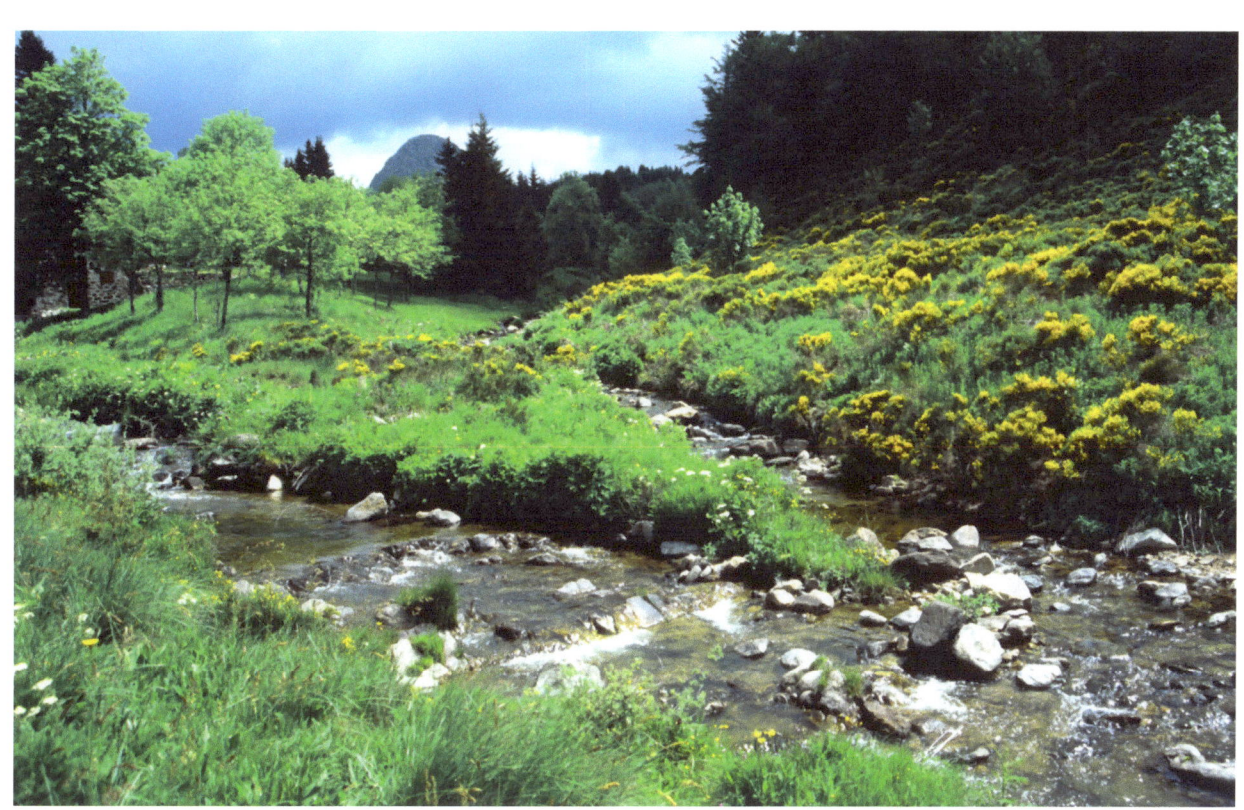

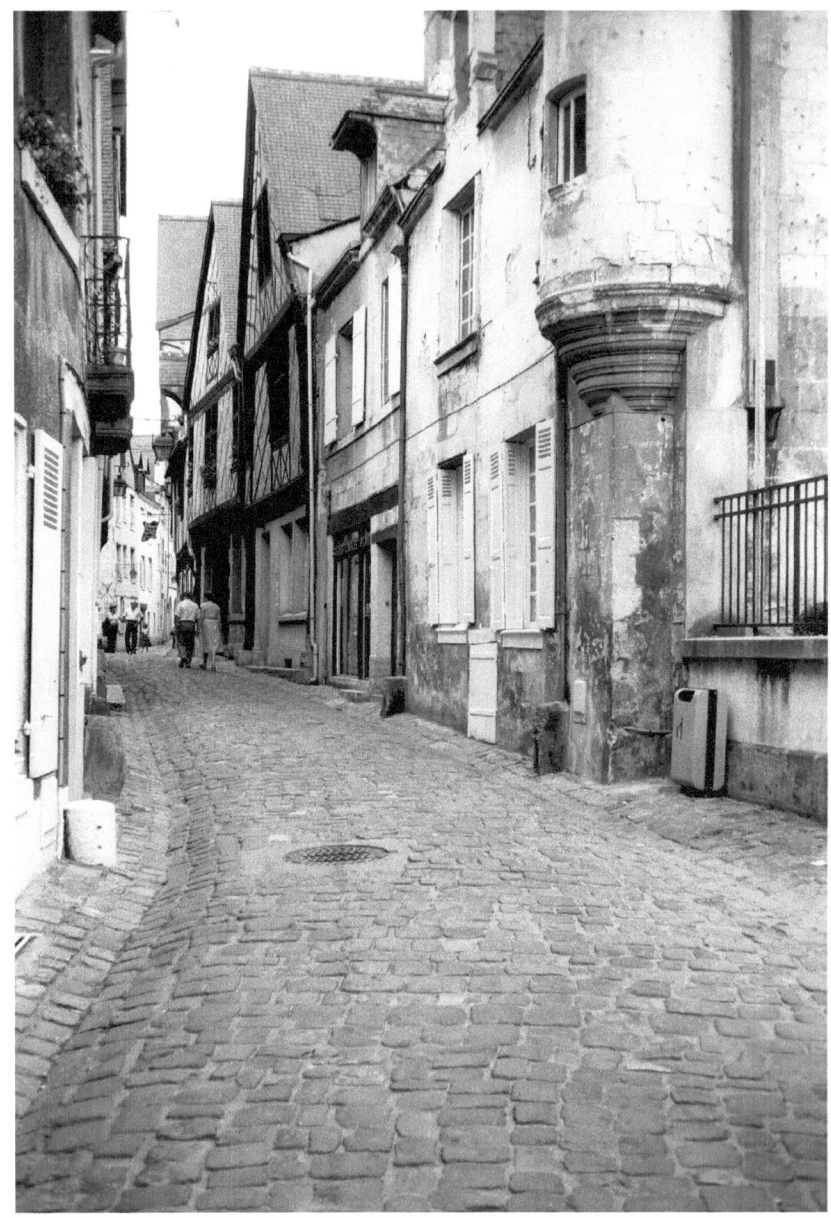

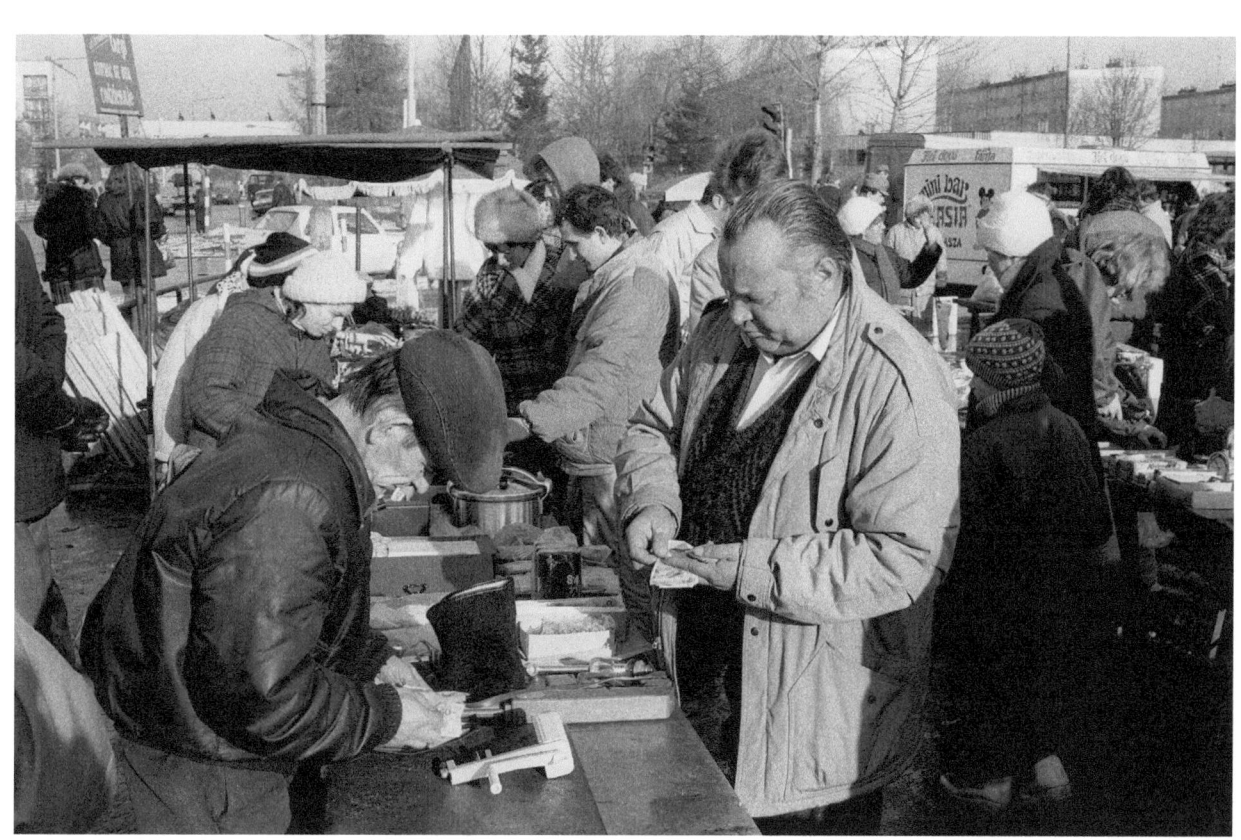

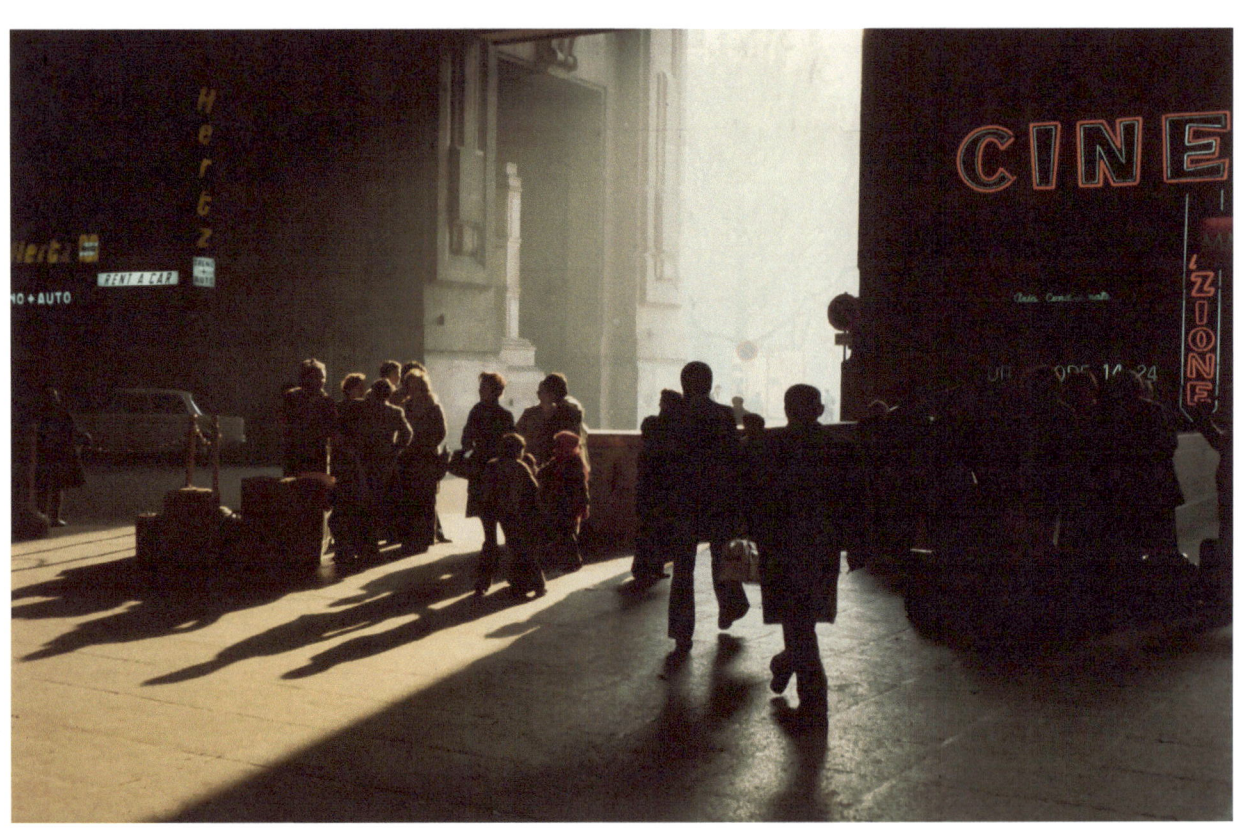

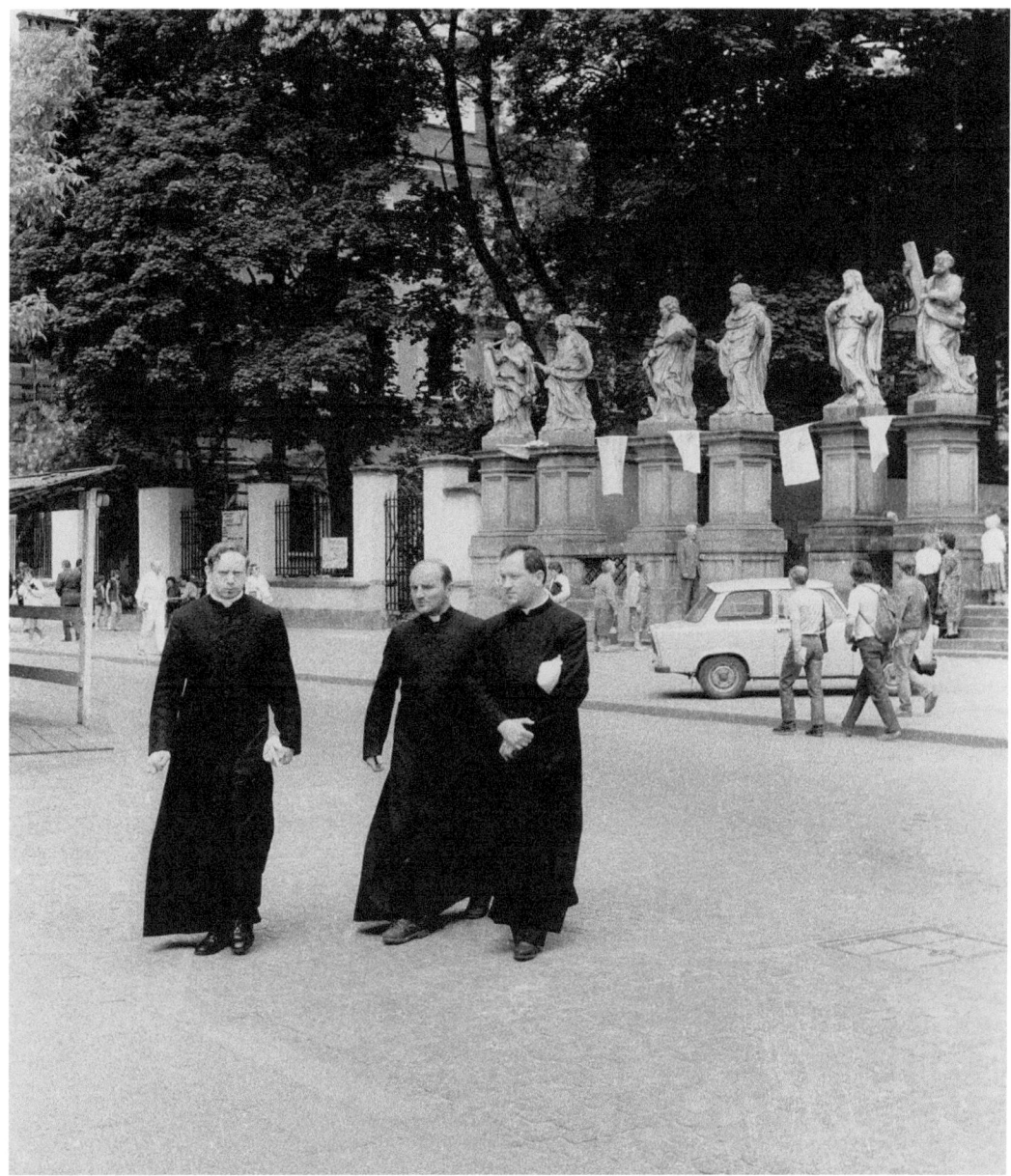

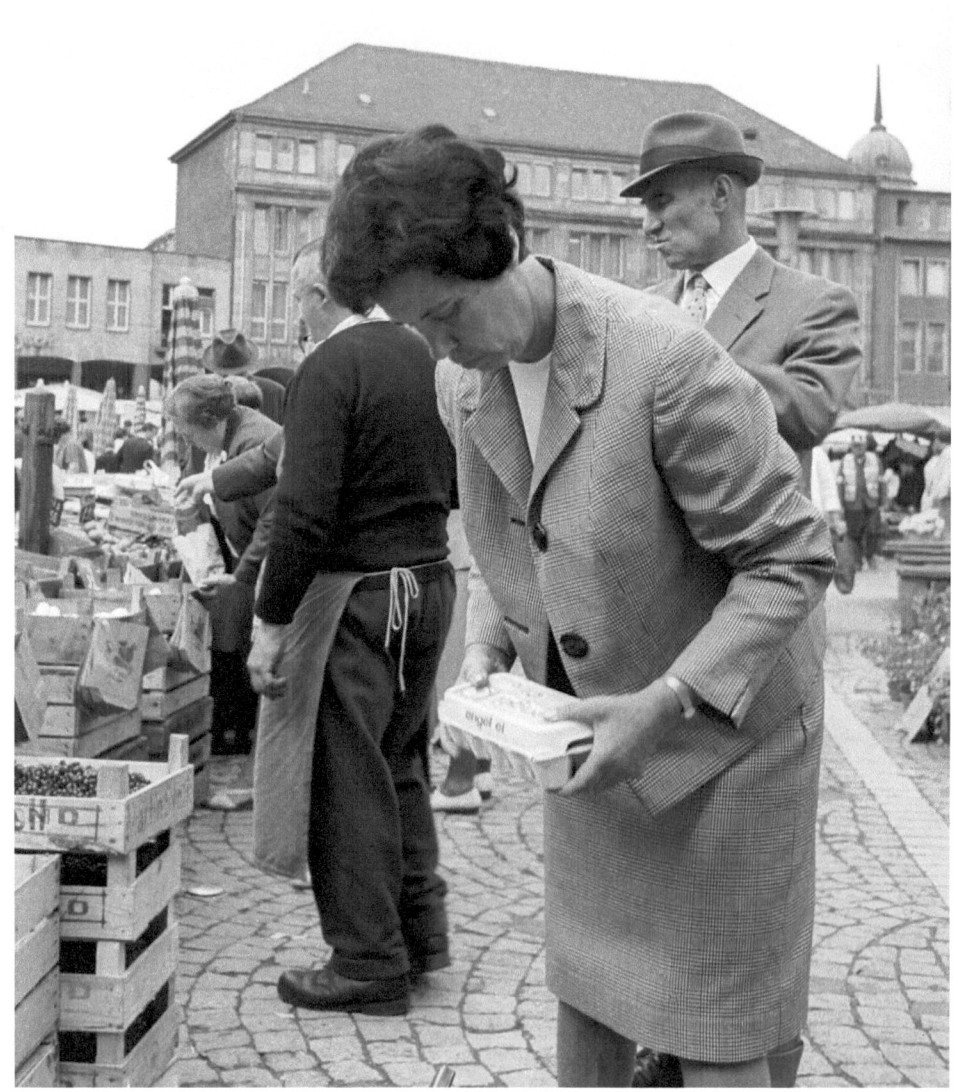

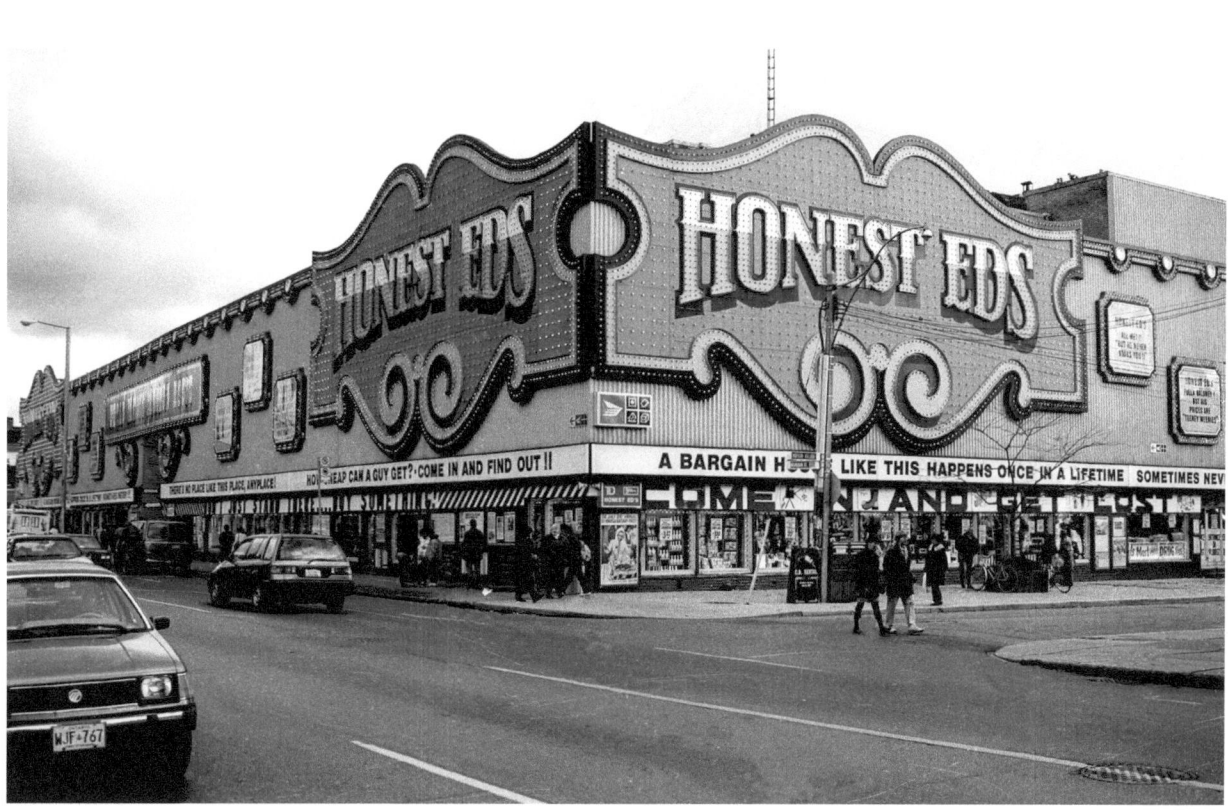

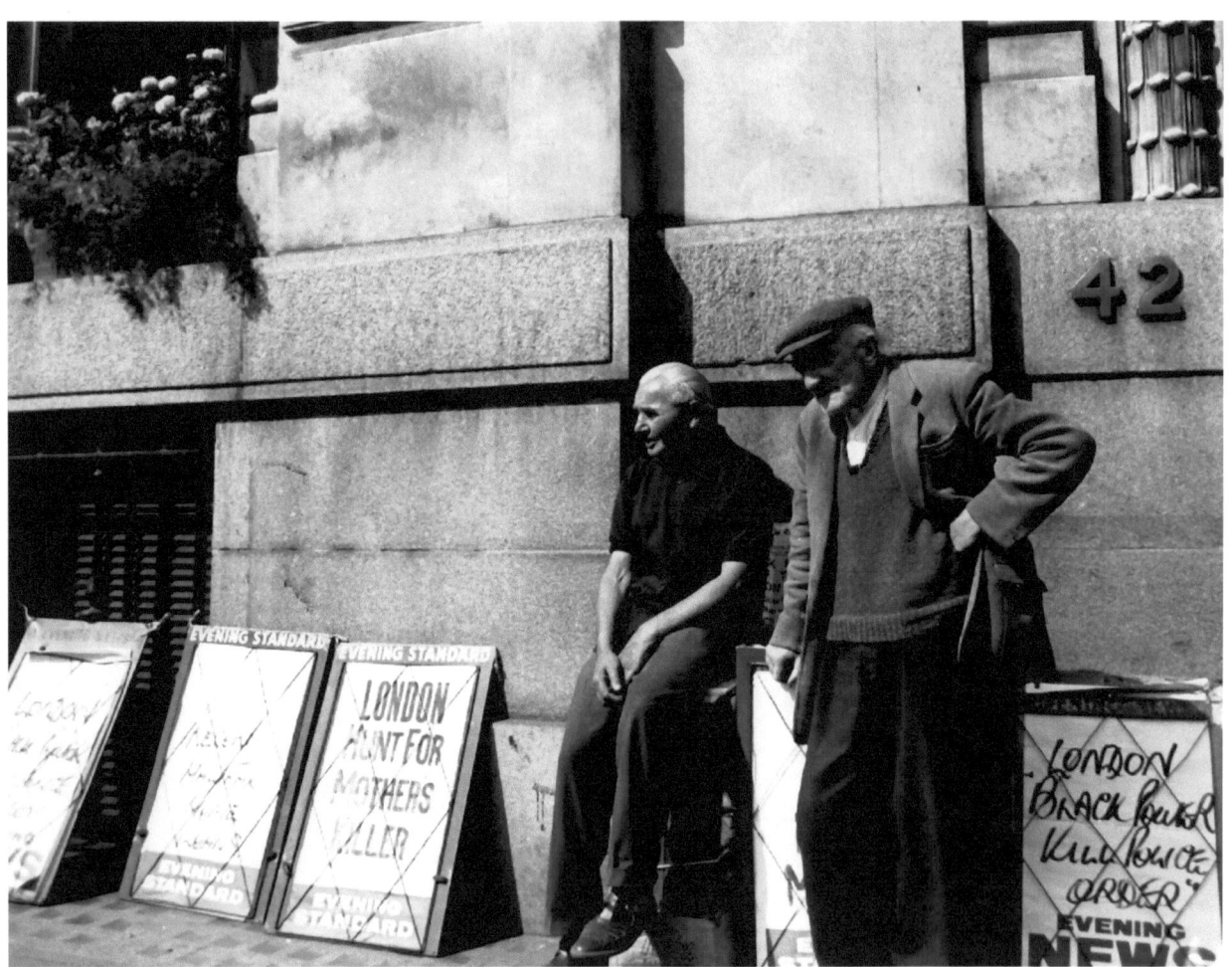

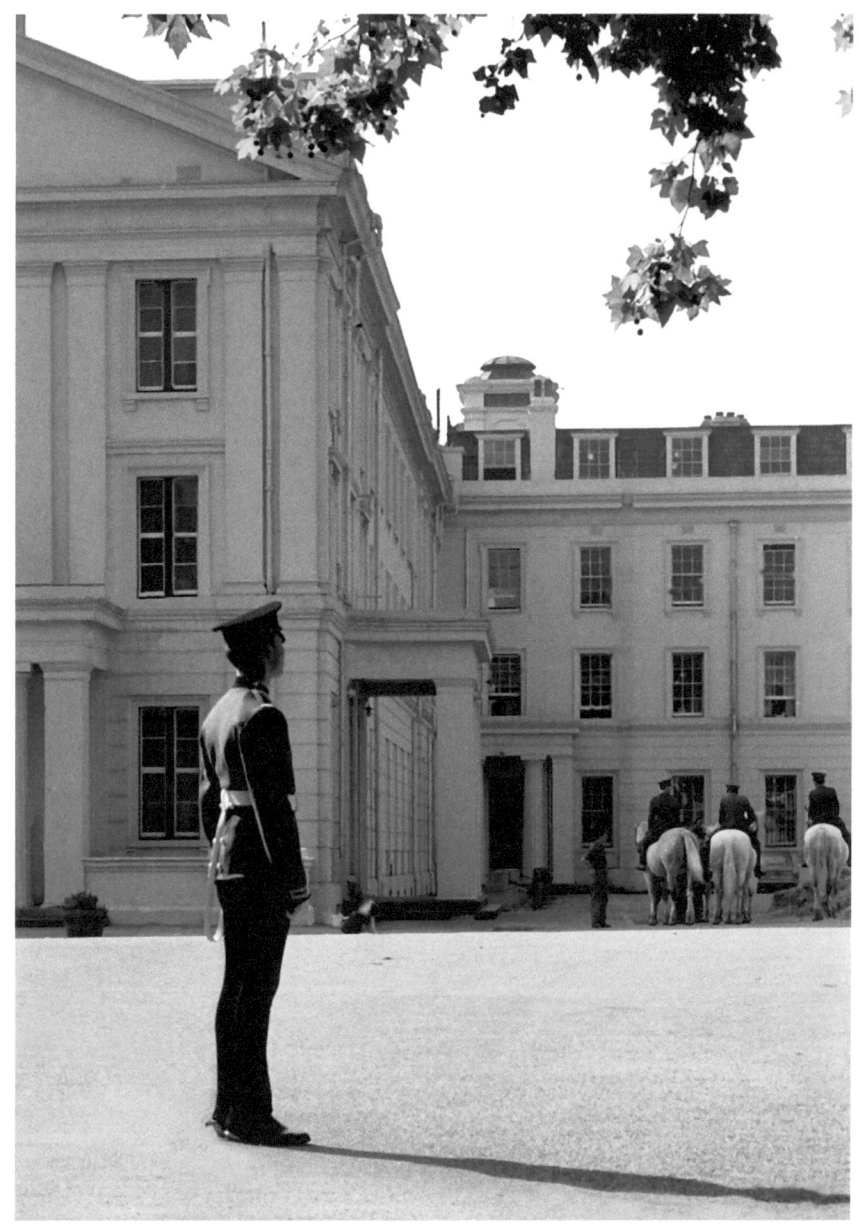

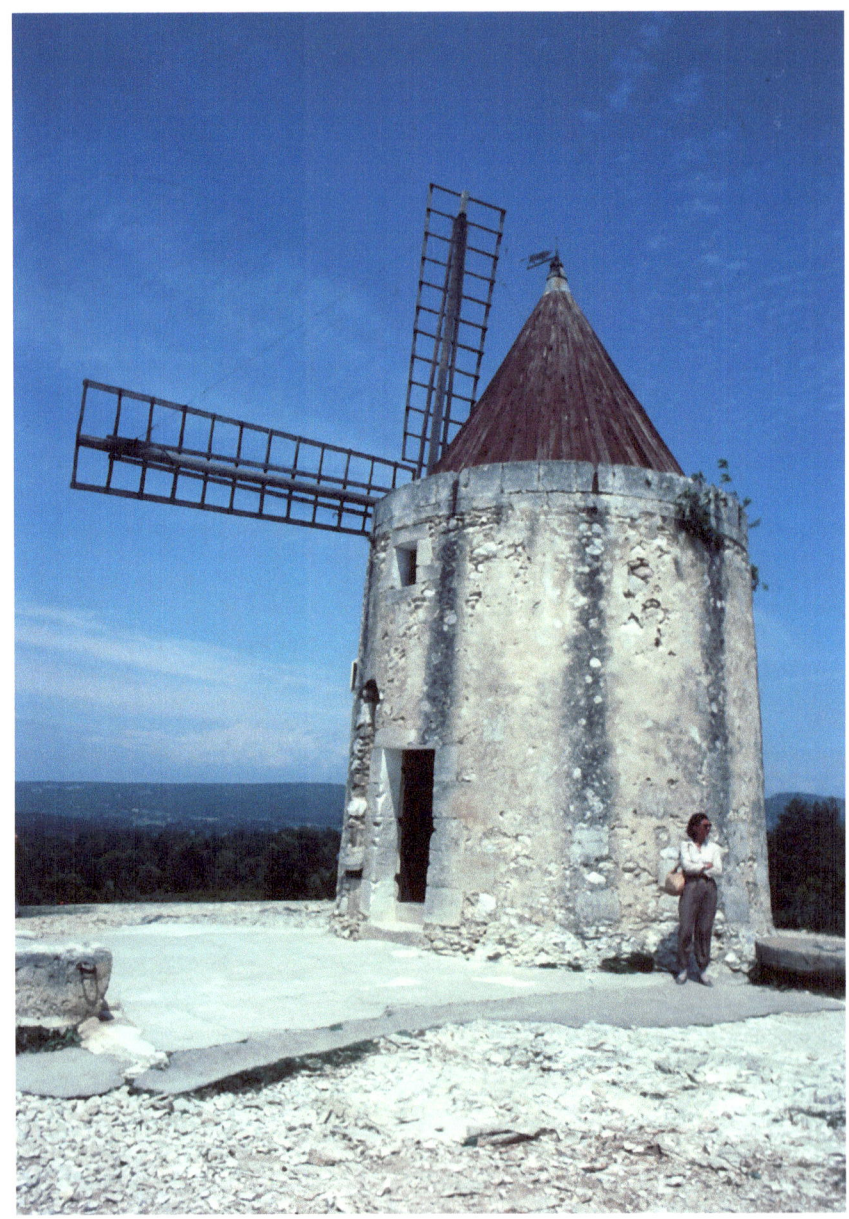

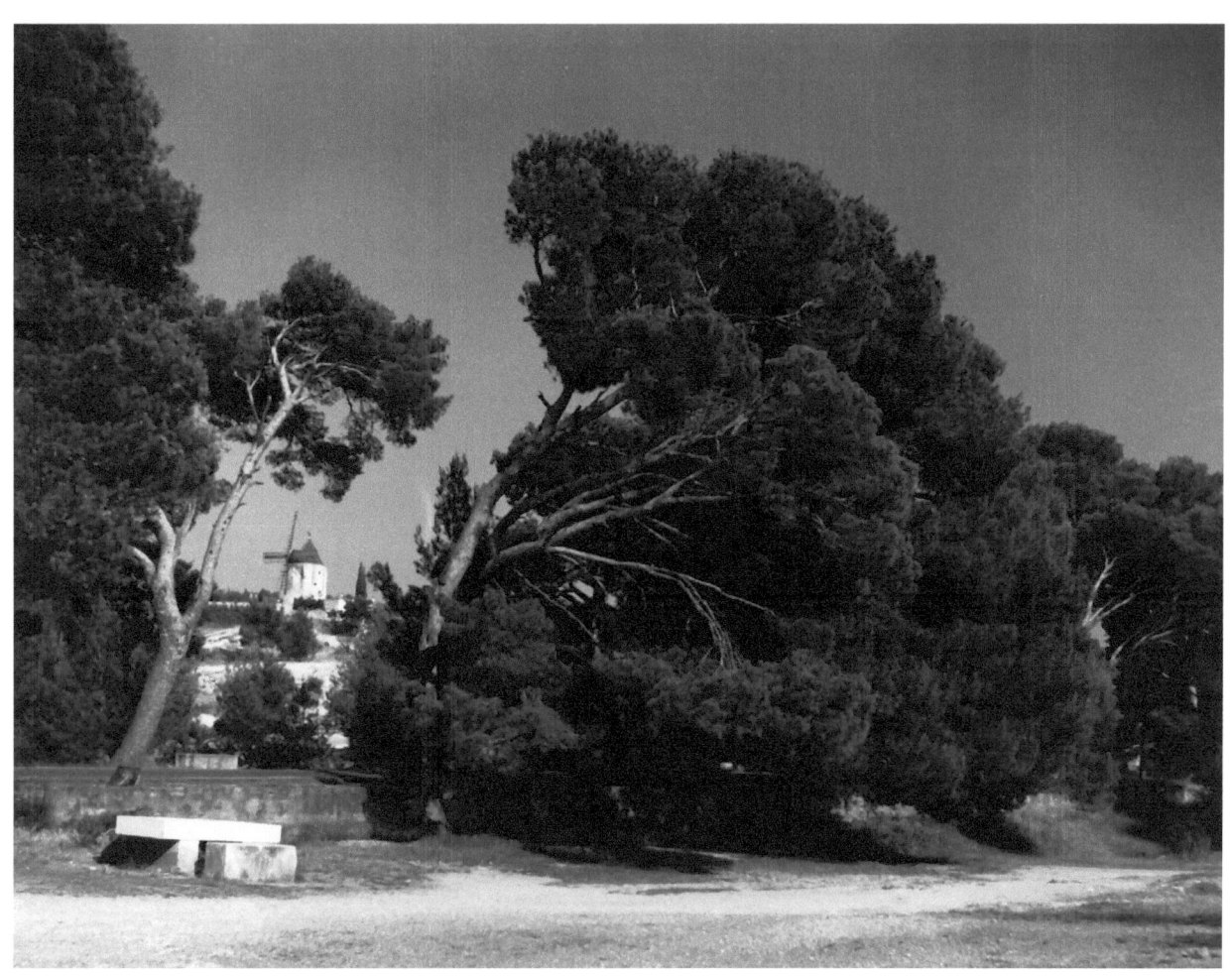

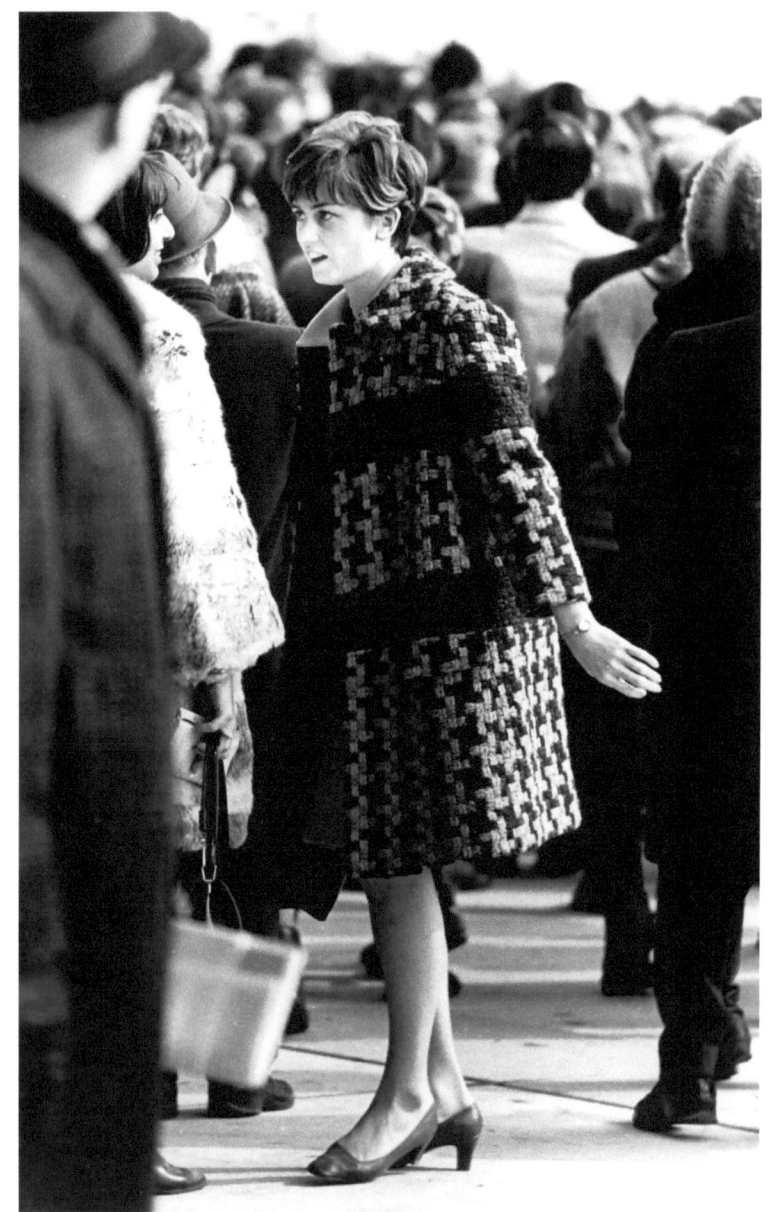

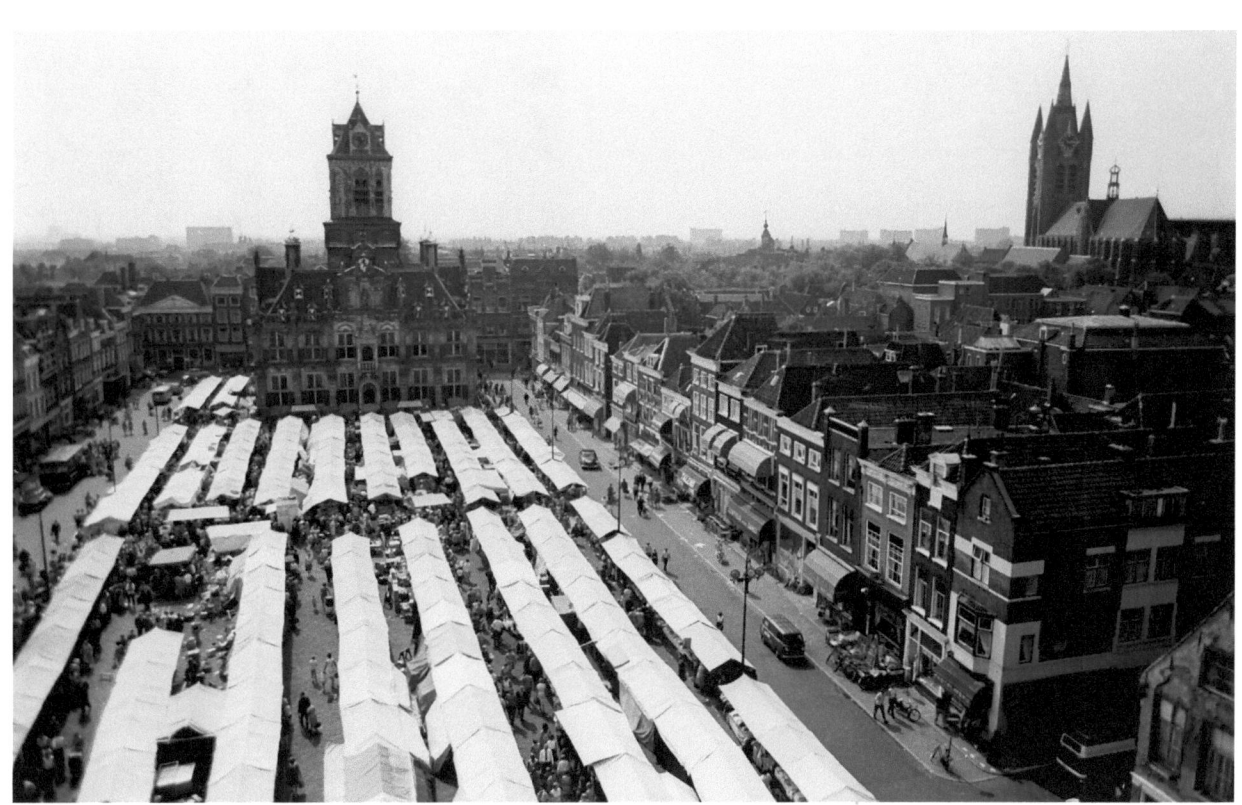

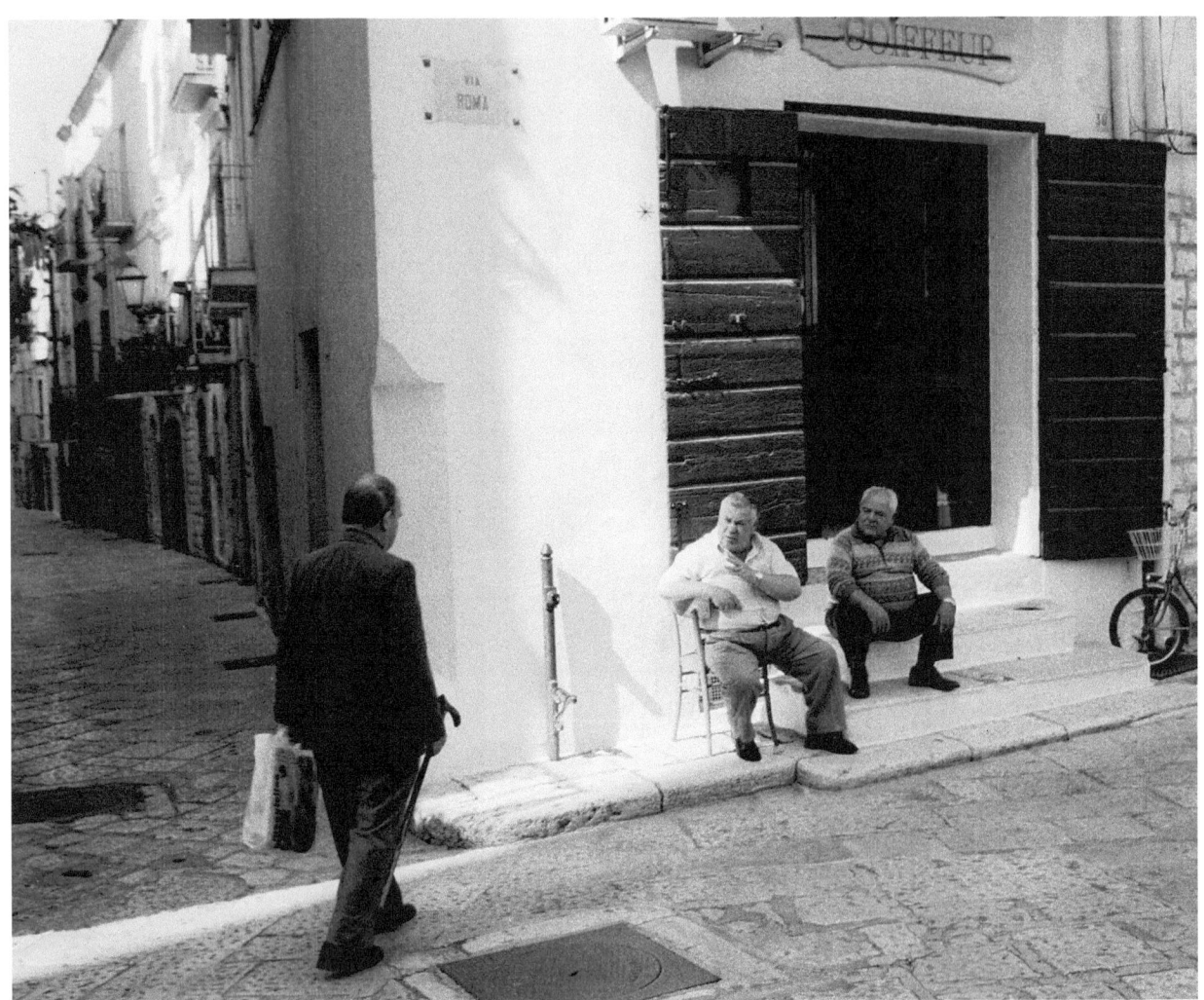

28

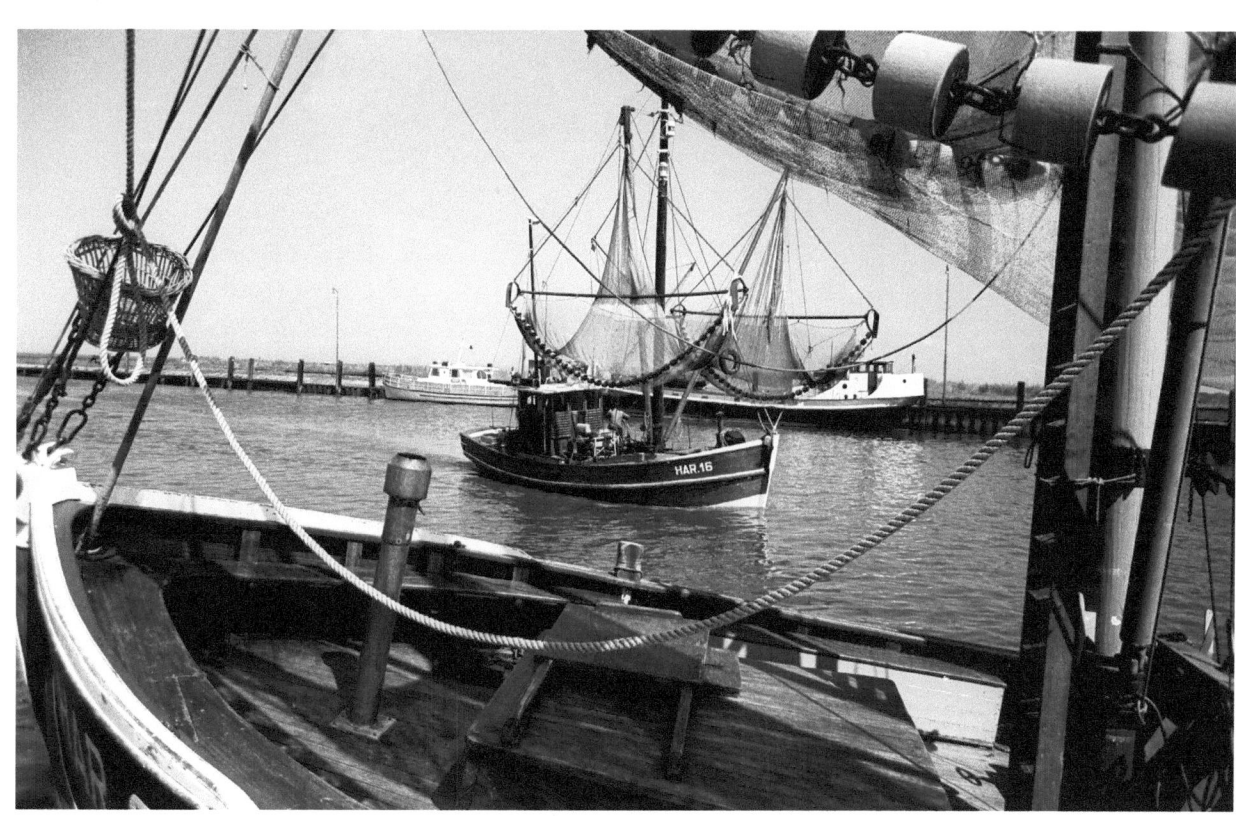

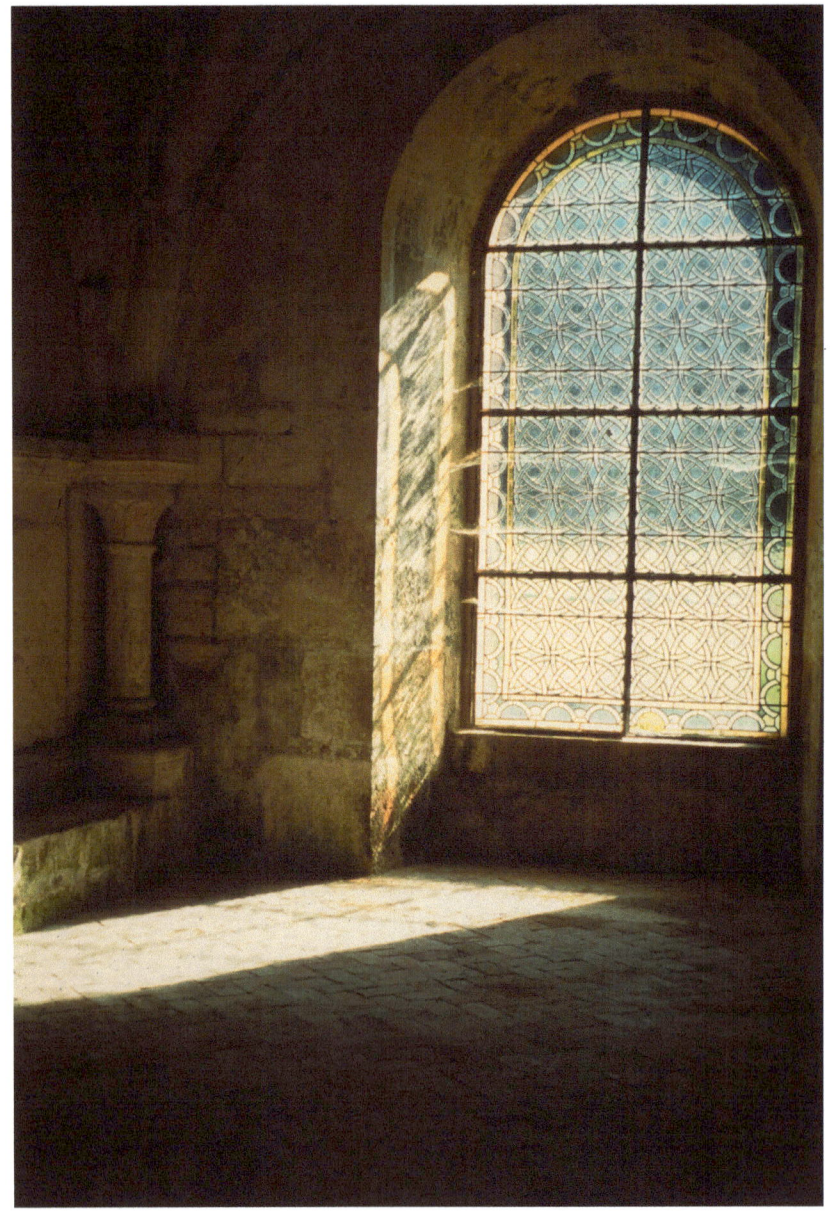

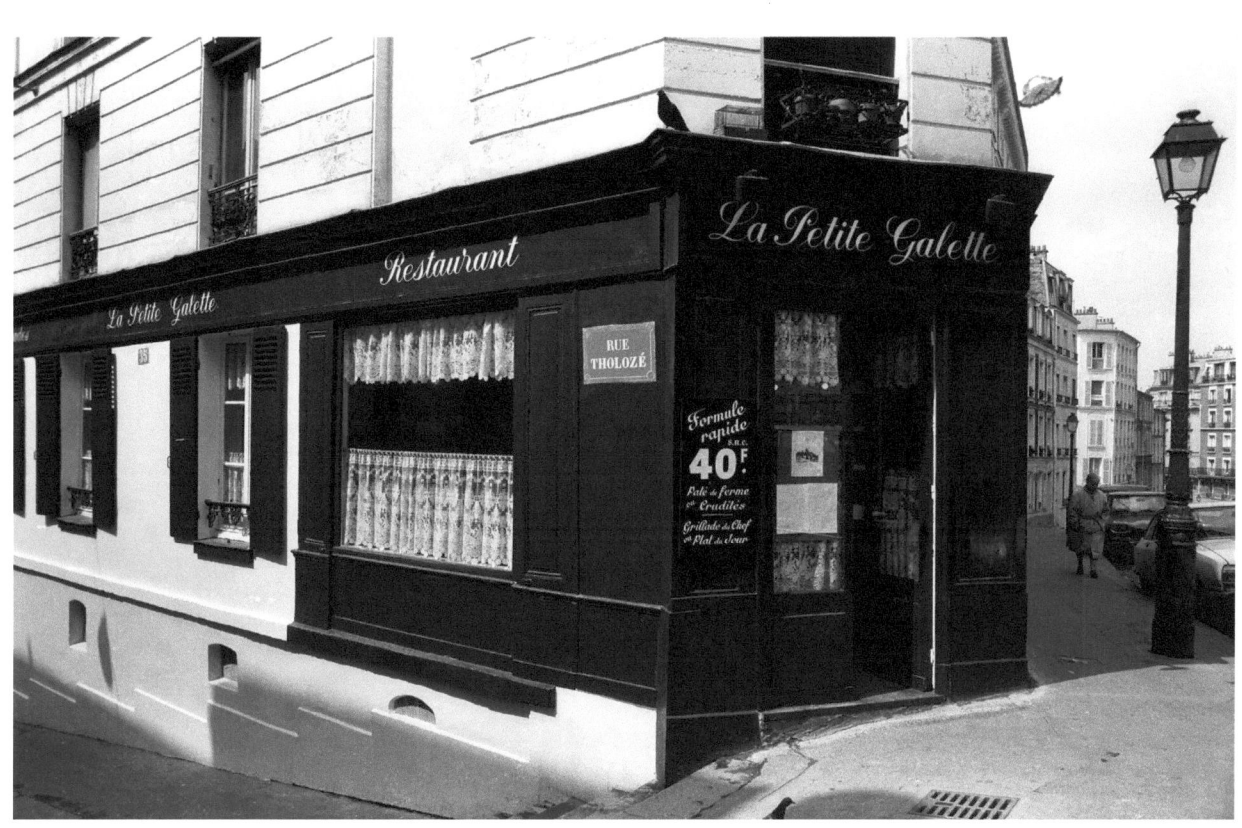

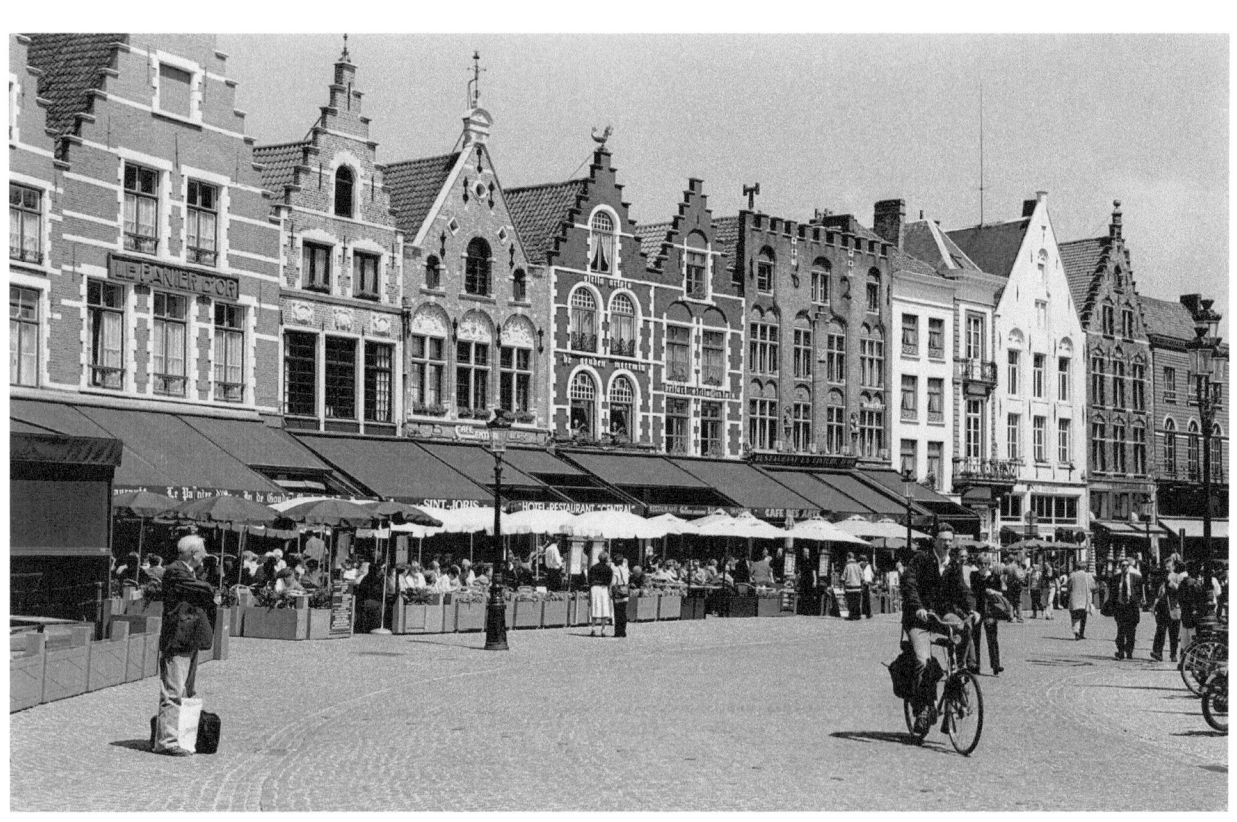

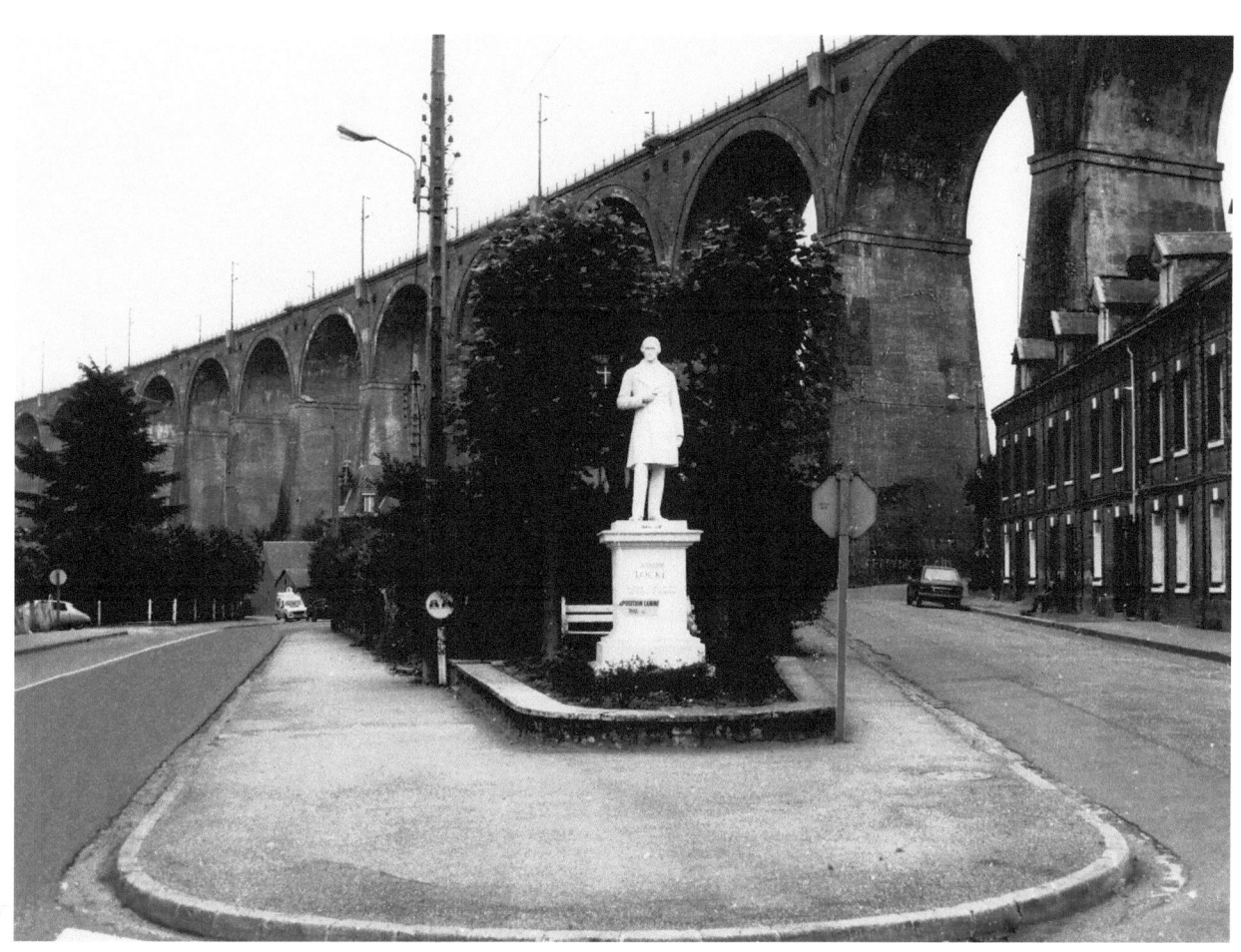

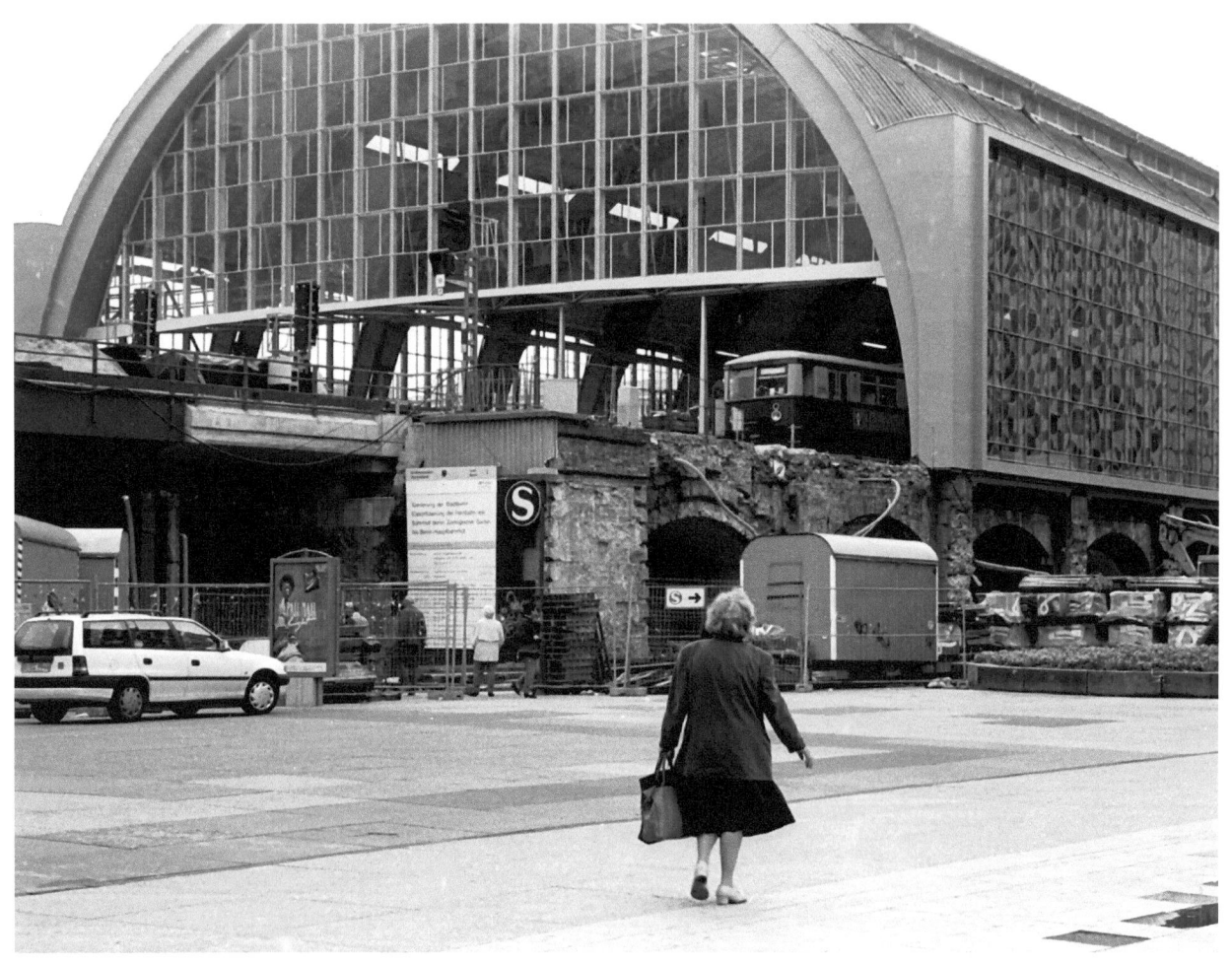

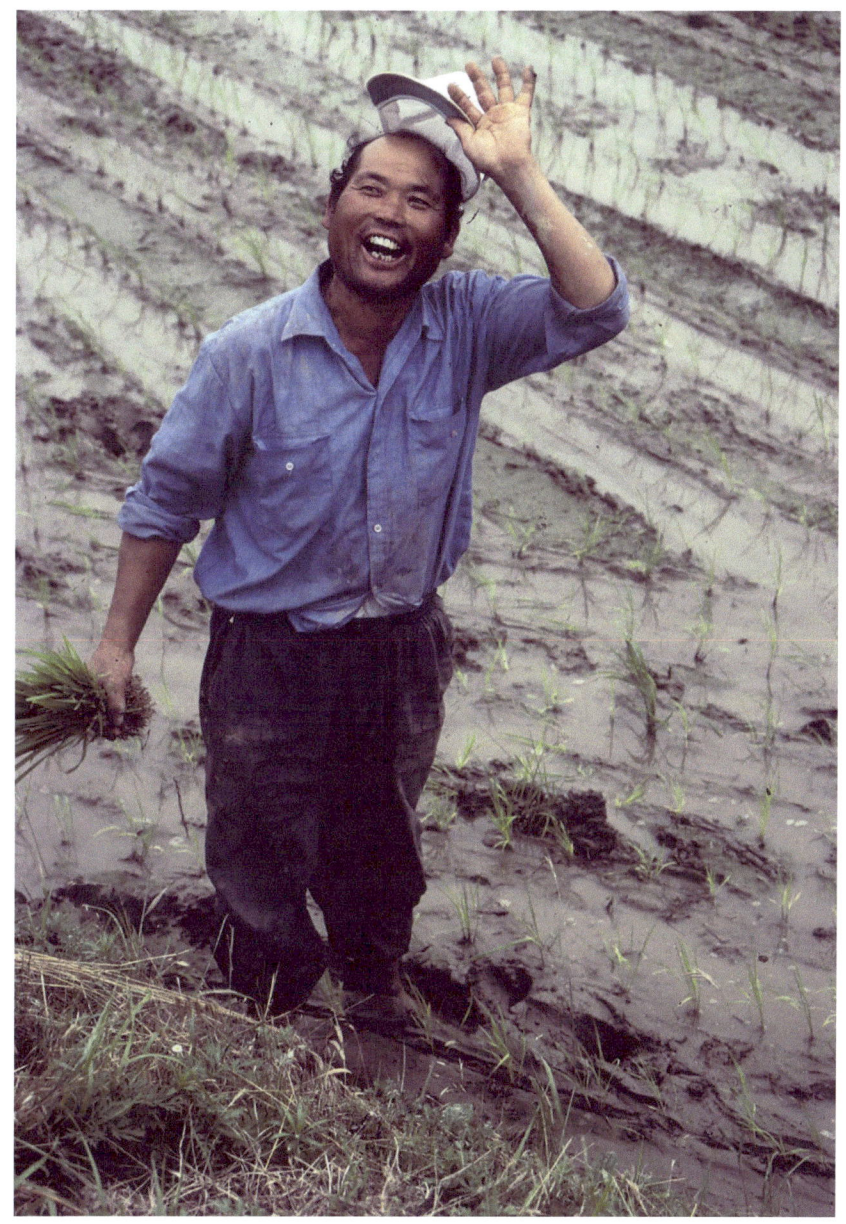

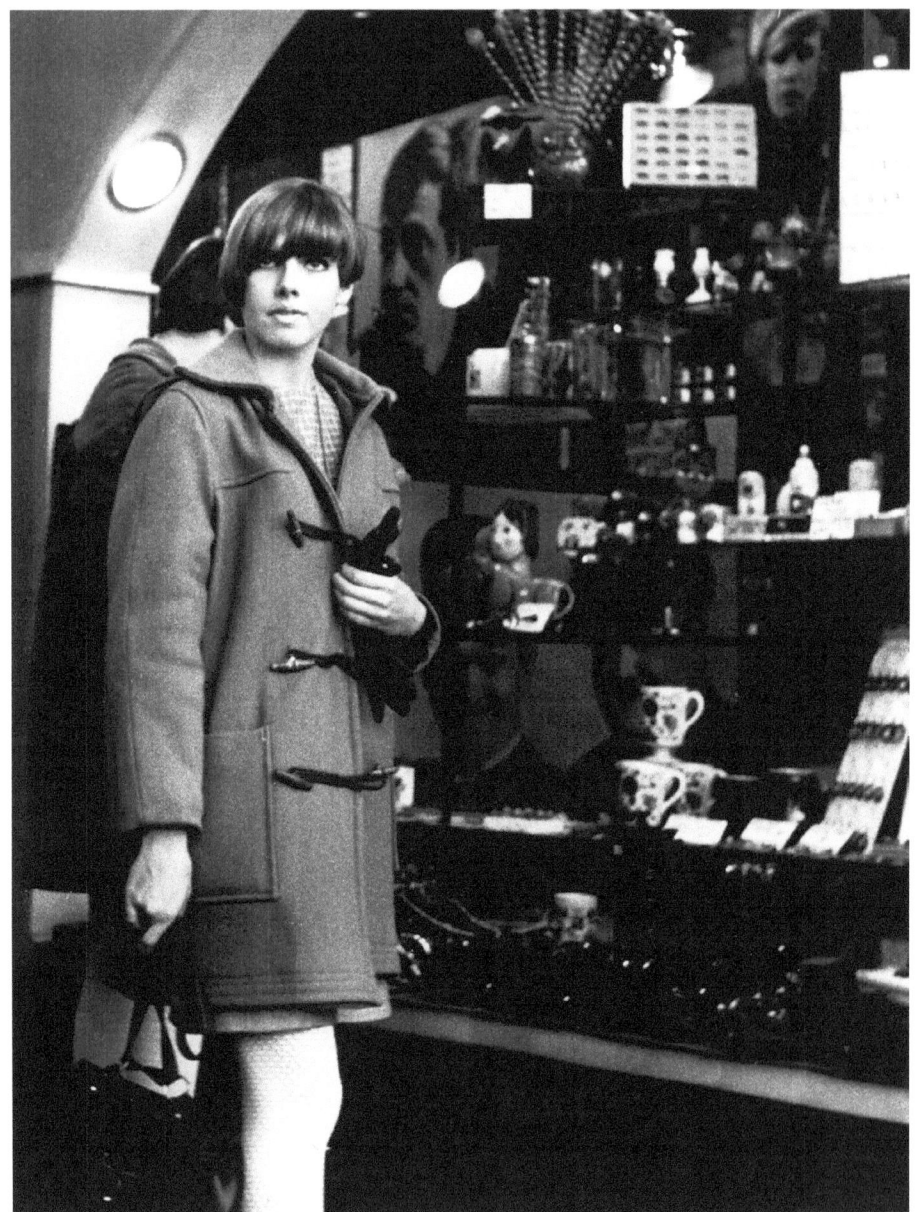

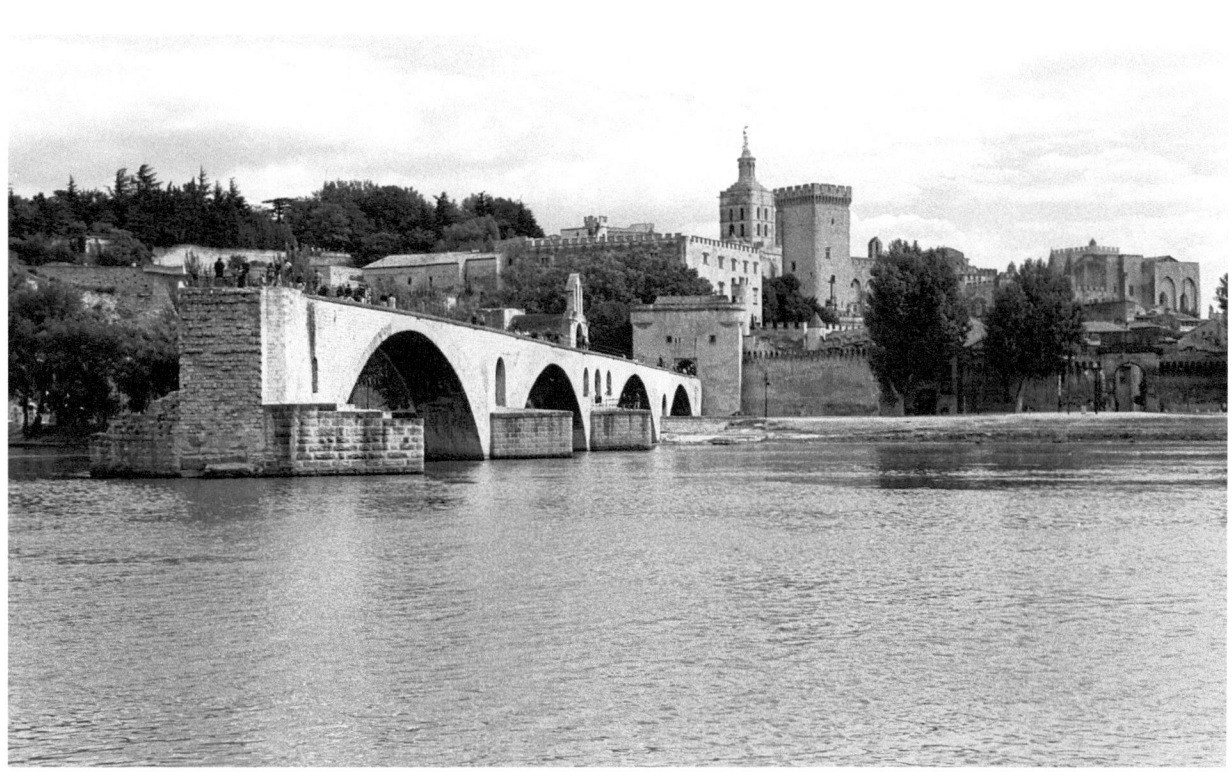

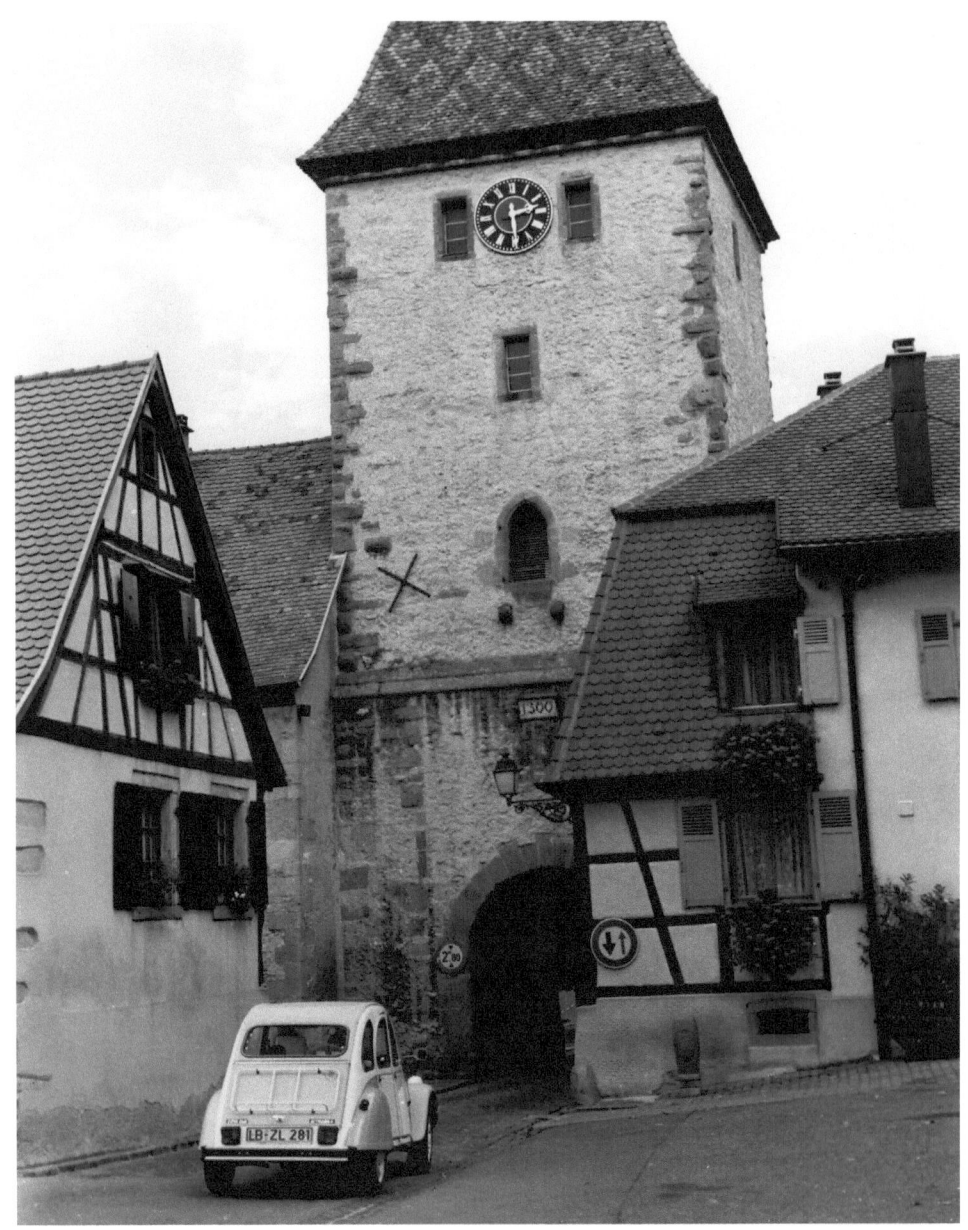

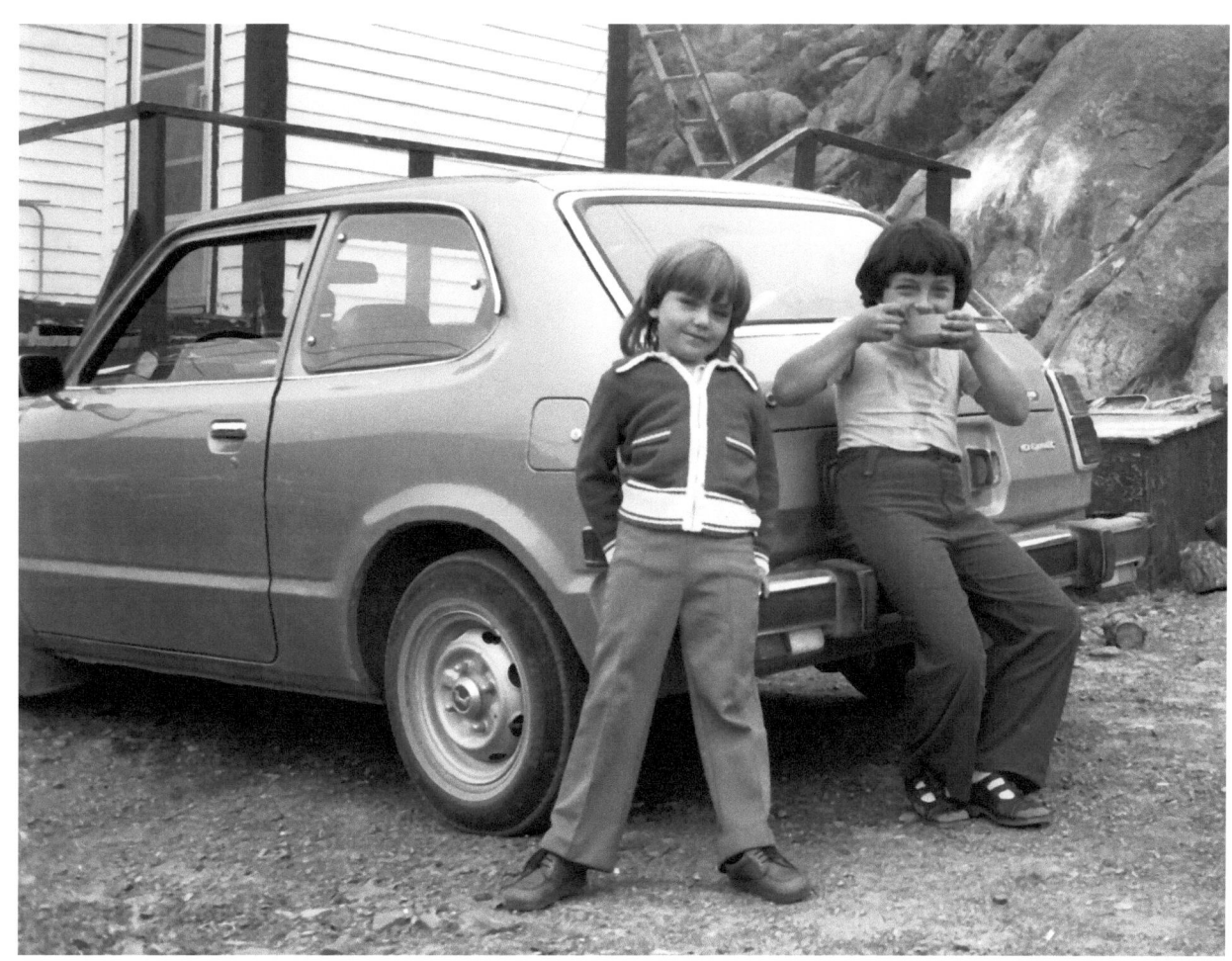

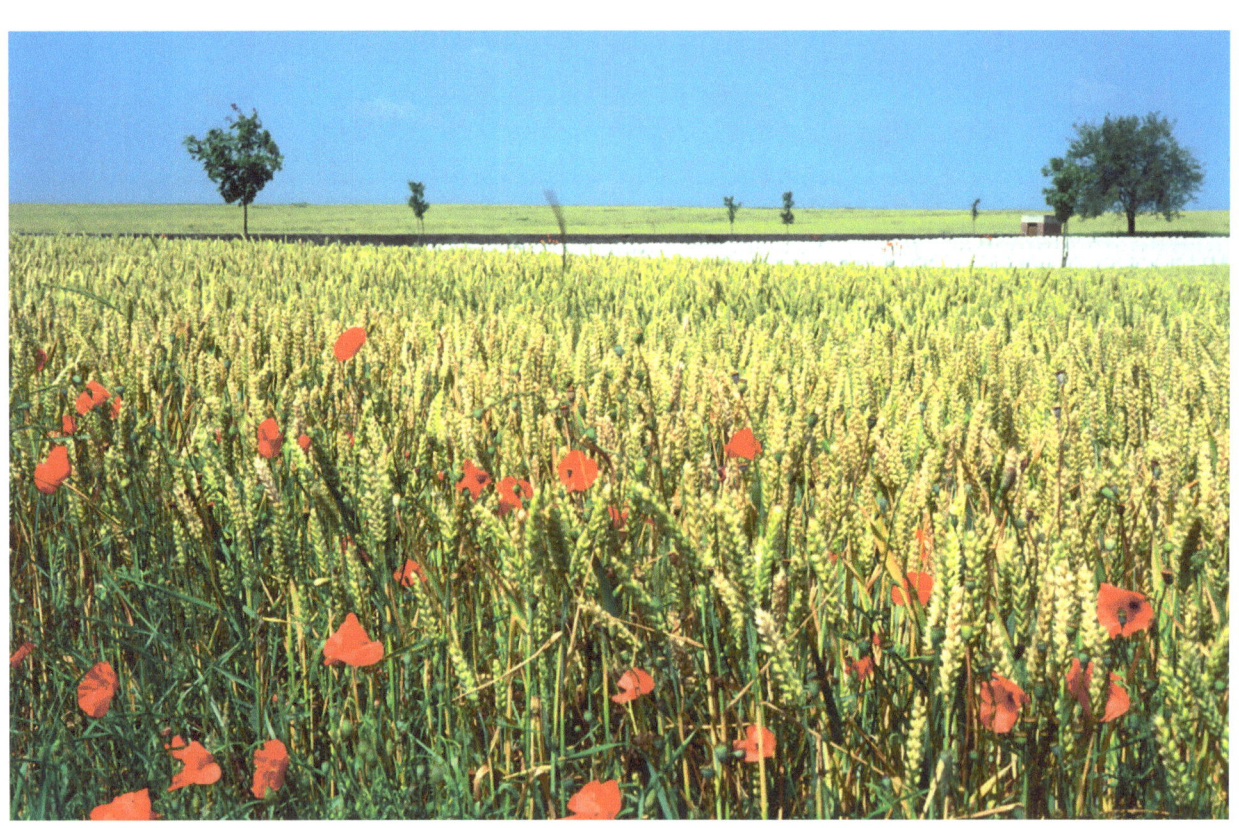

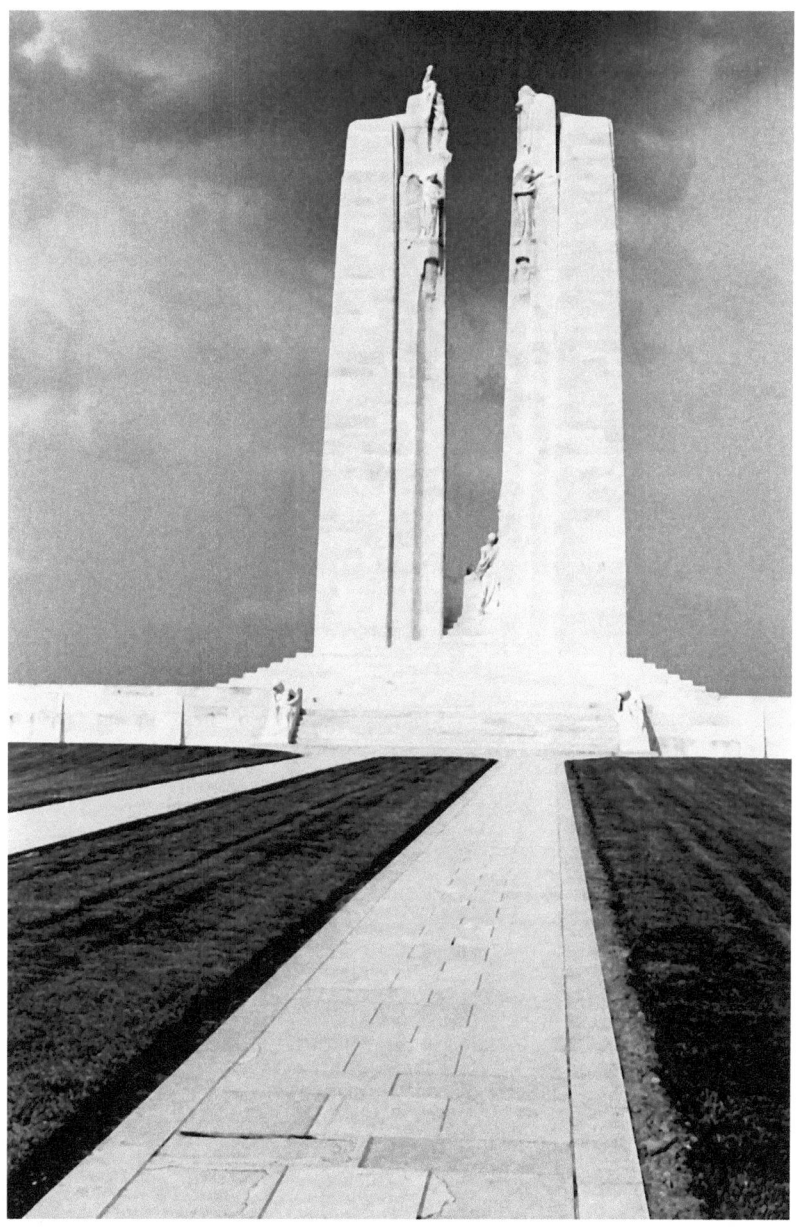

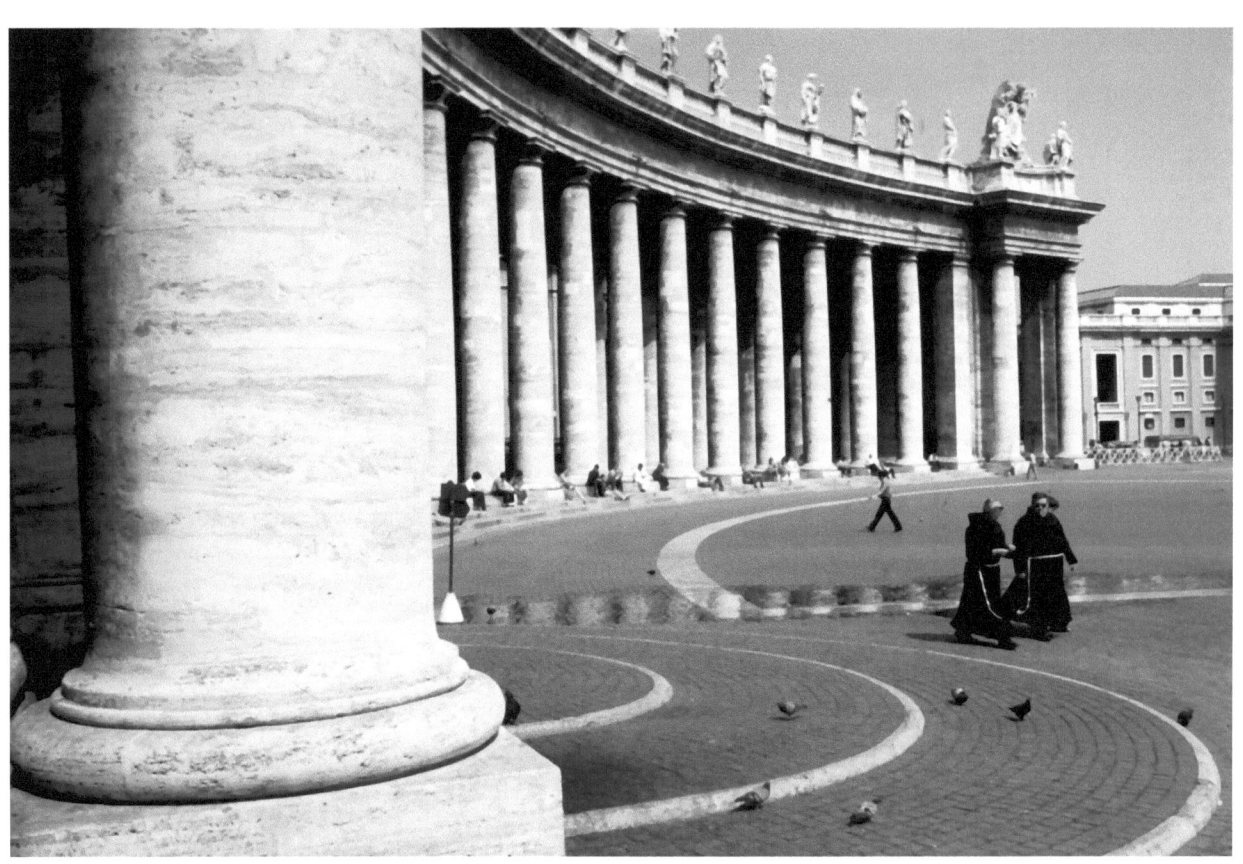

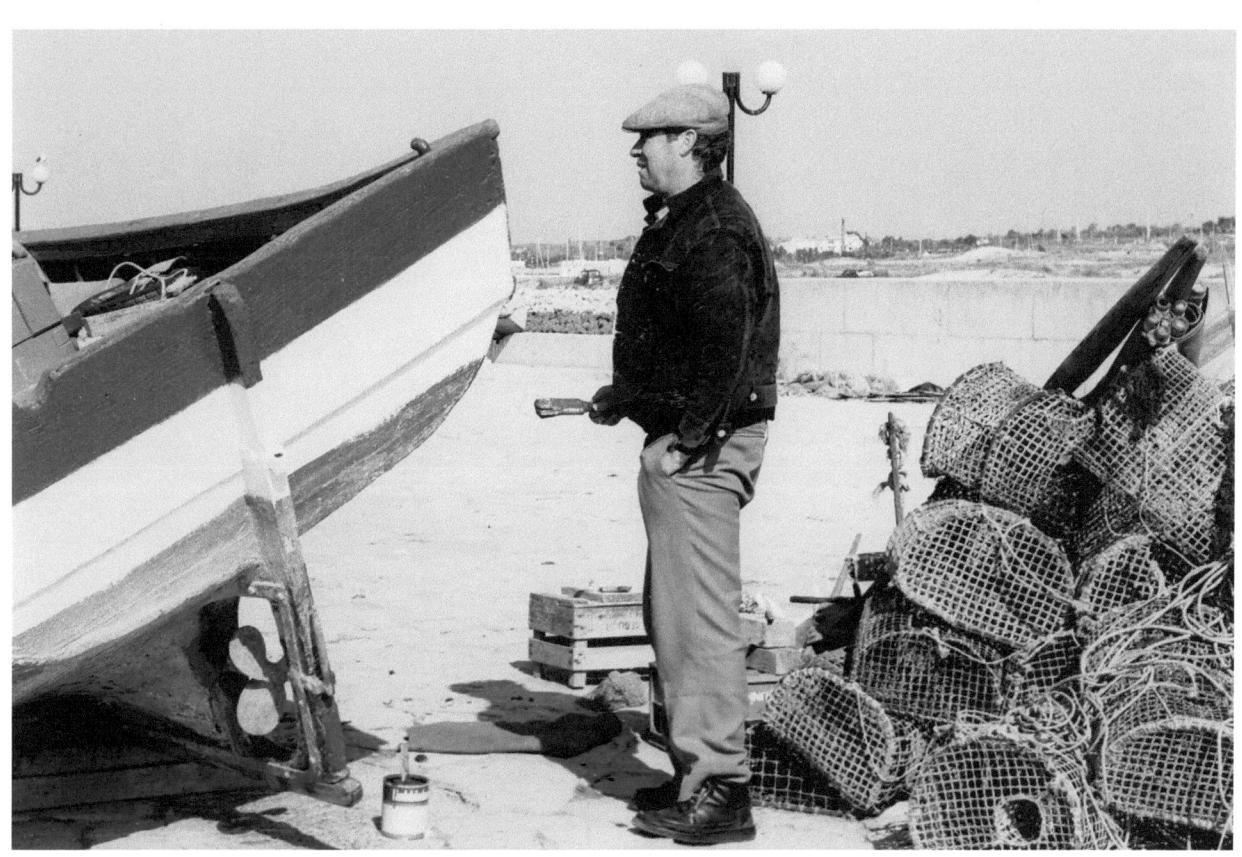

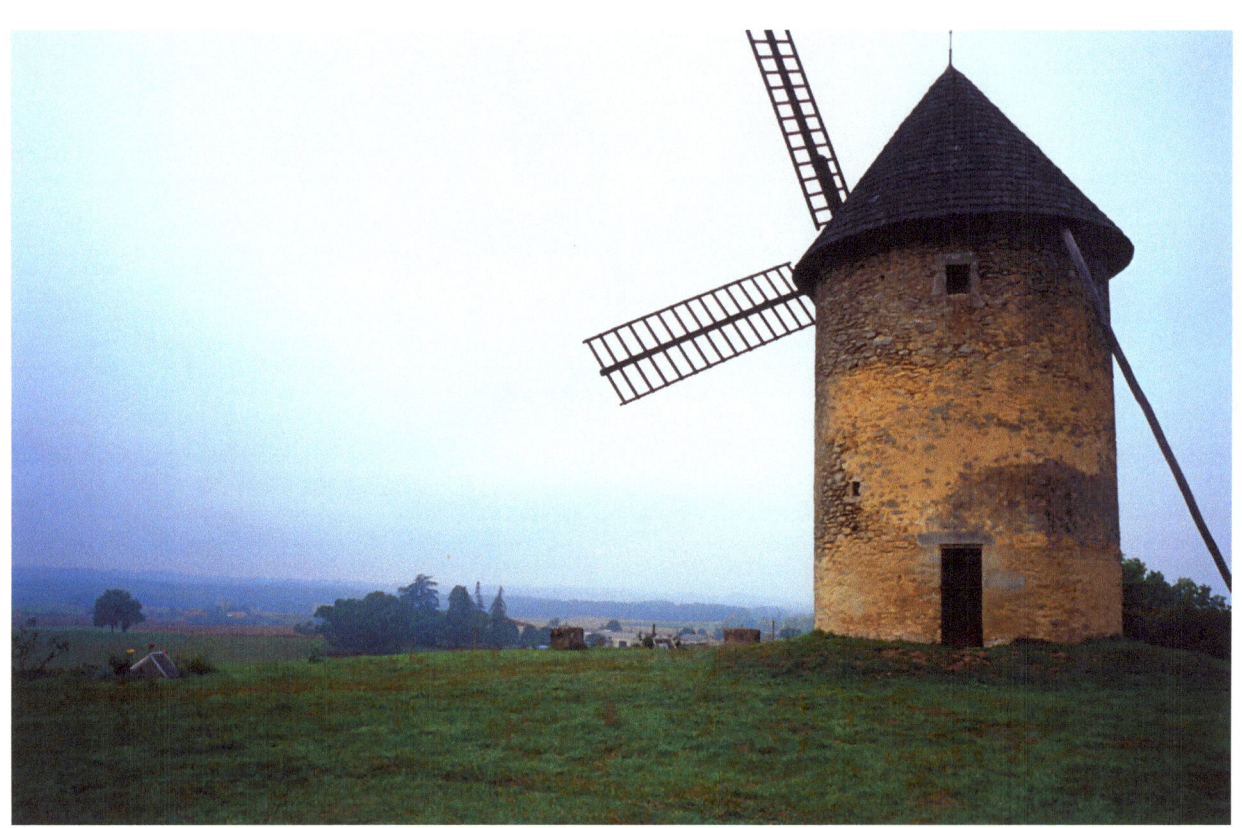

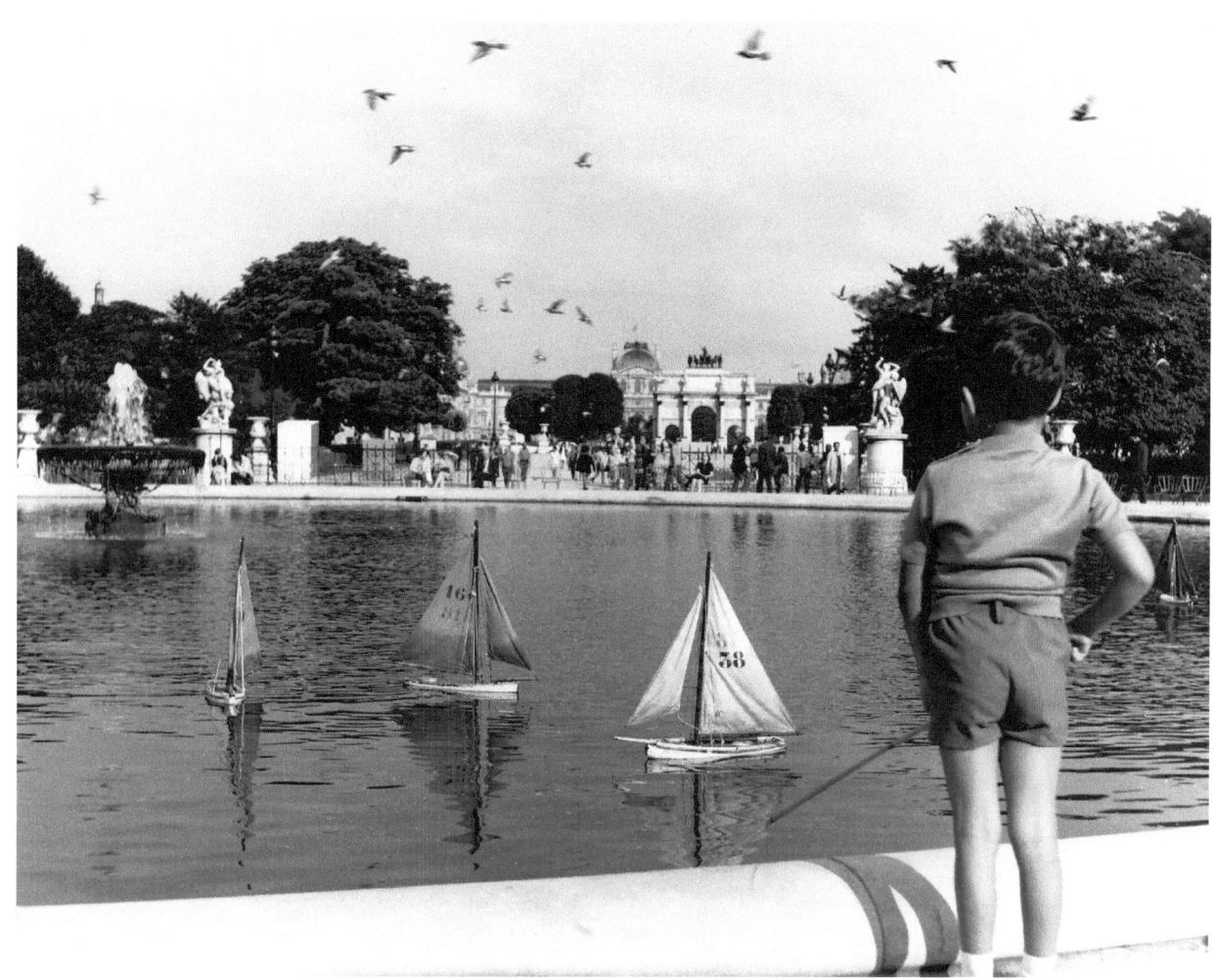

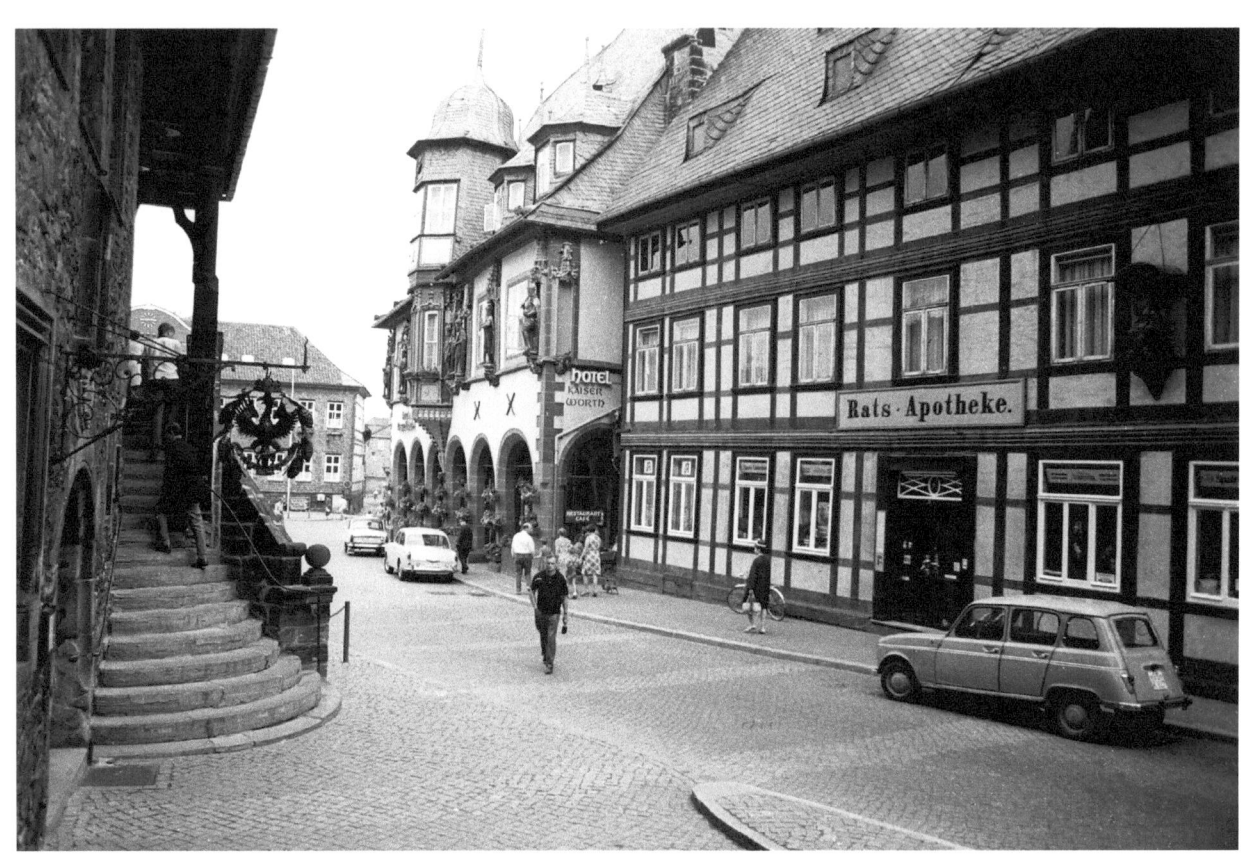

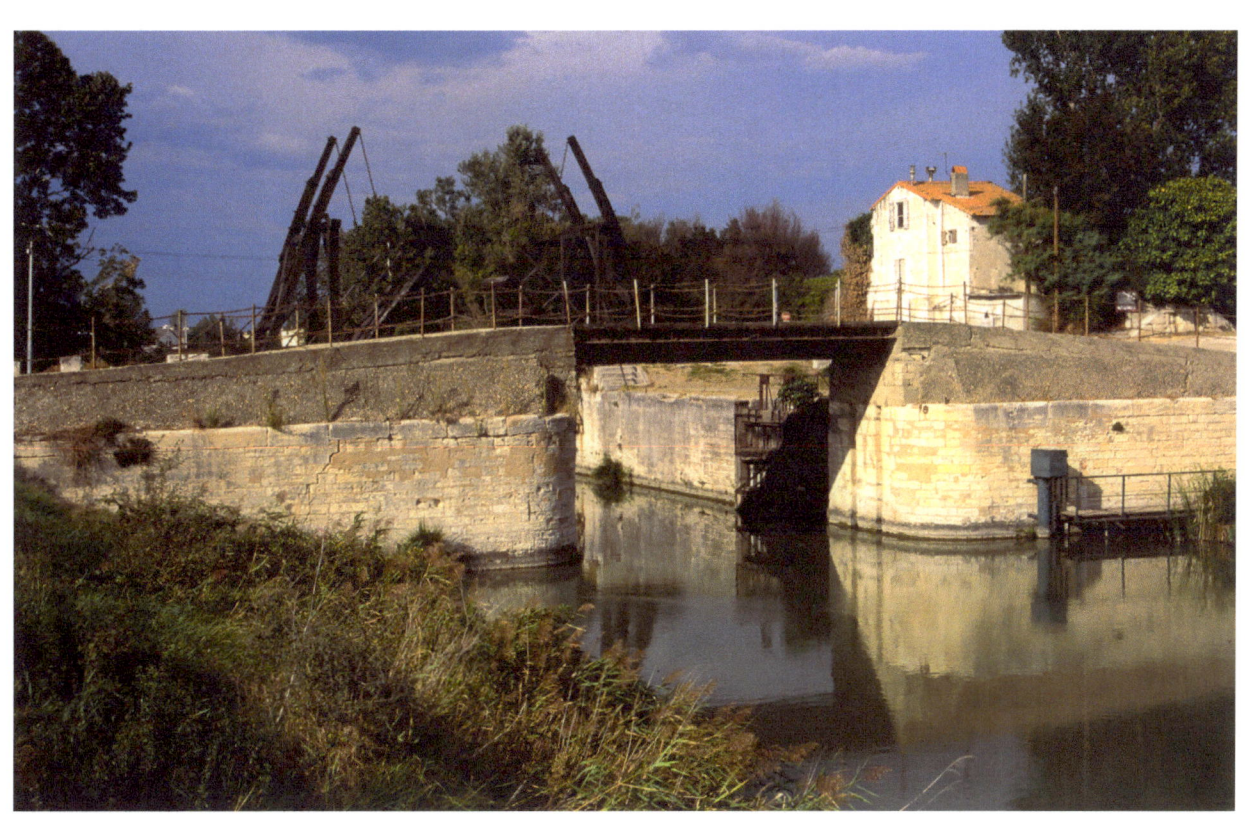

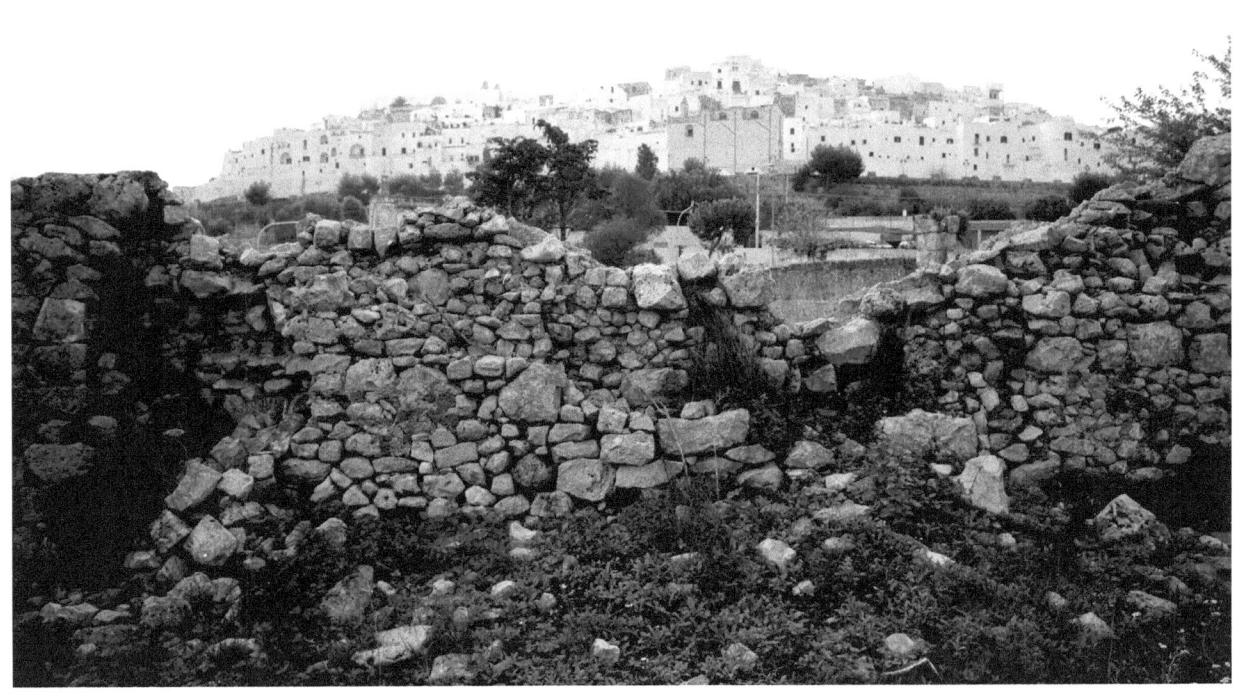

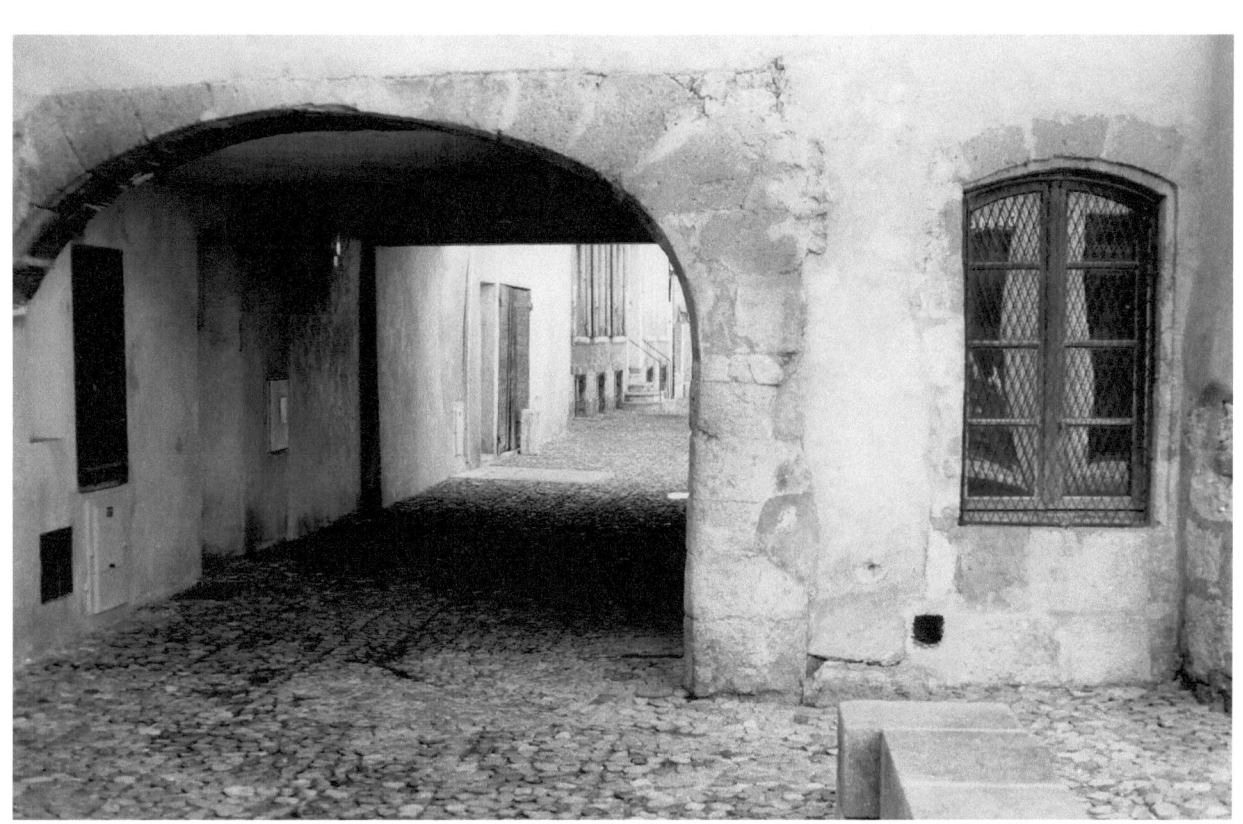

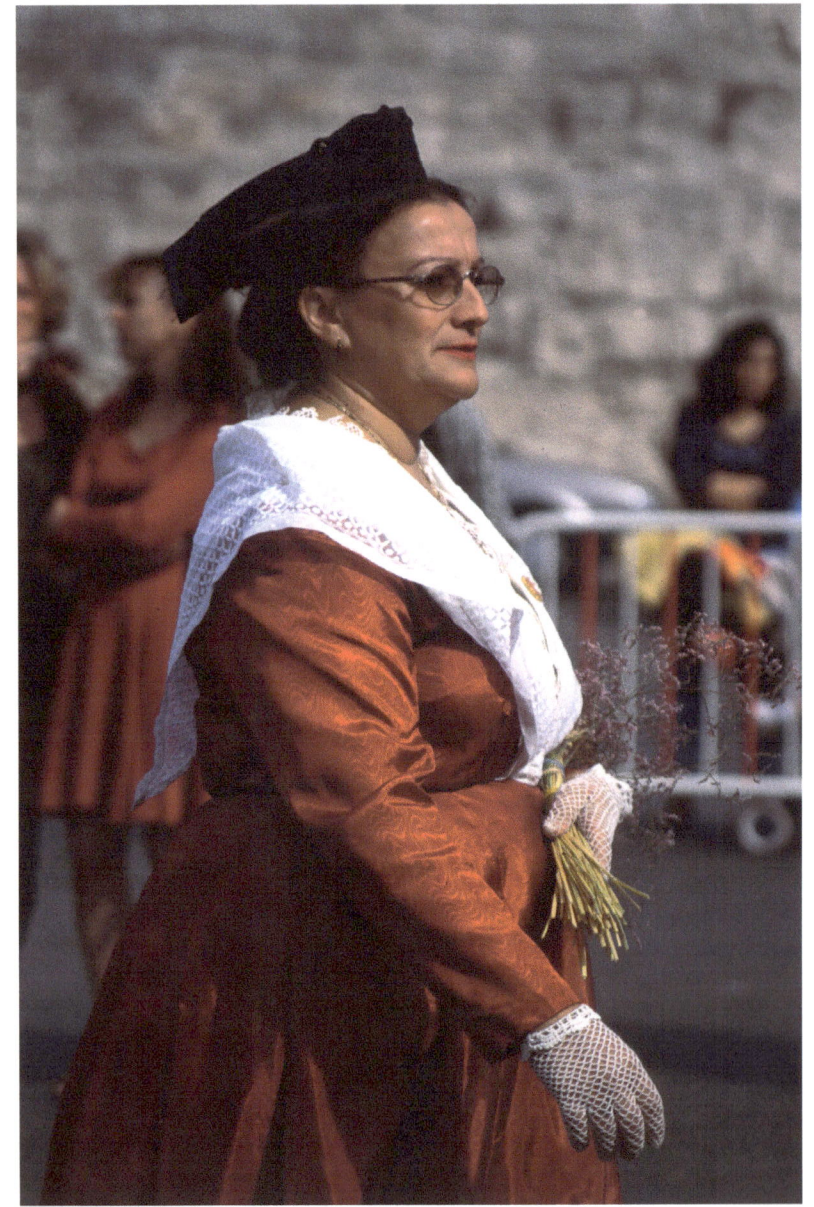

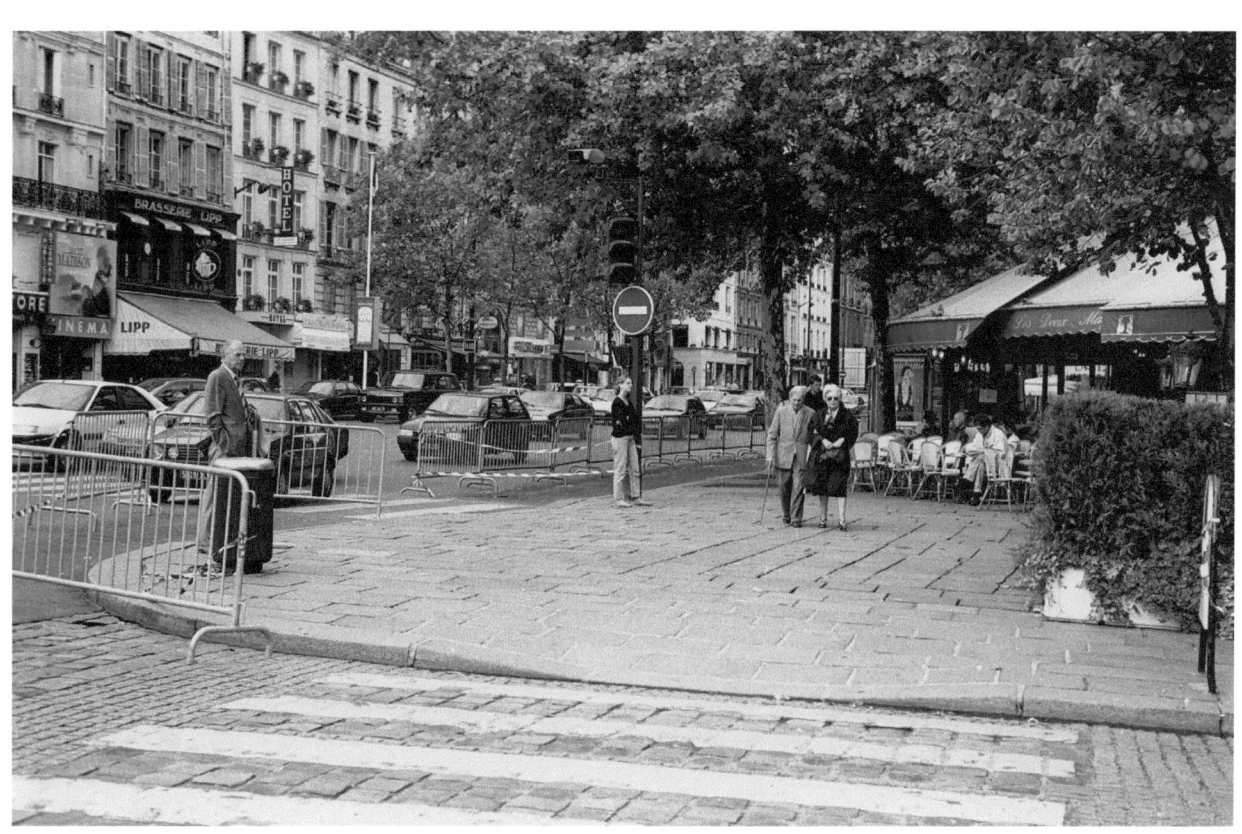

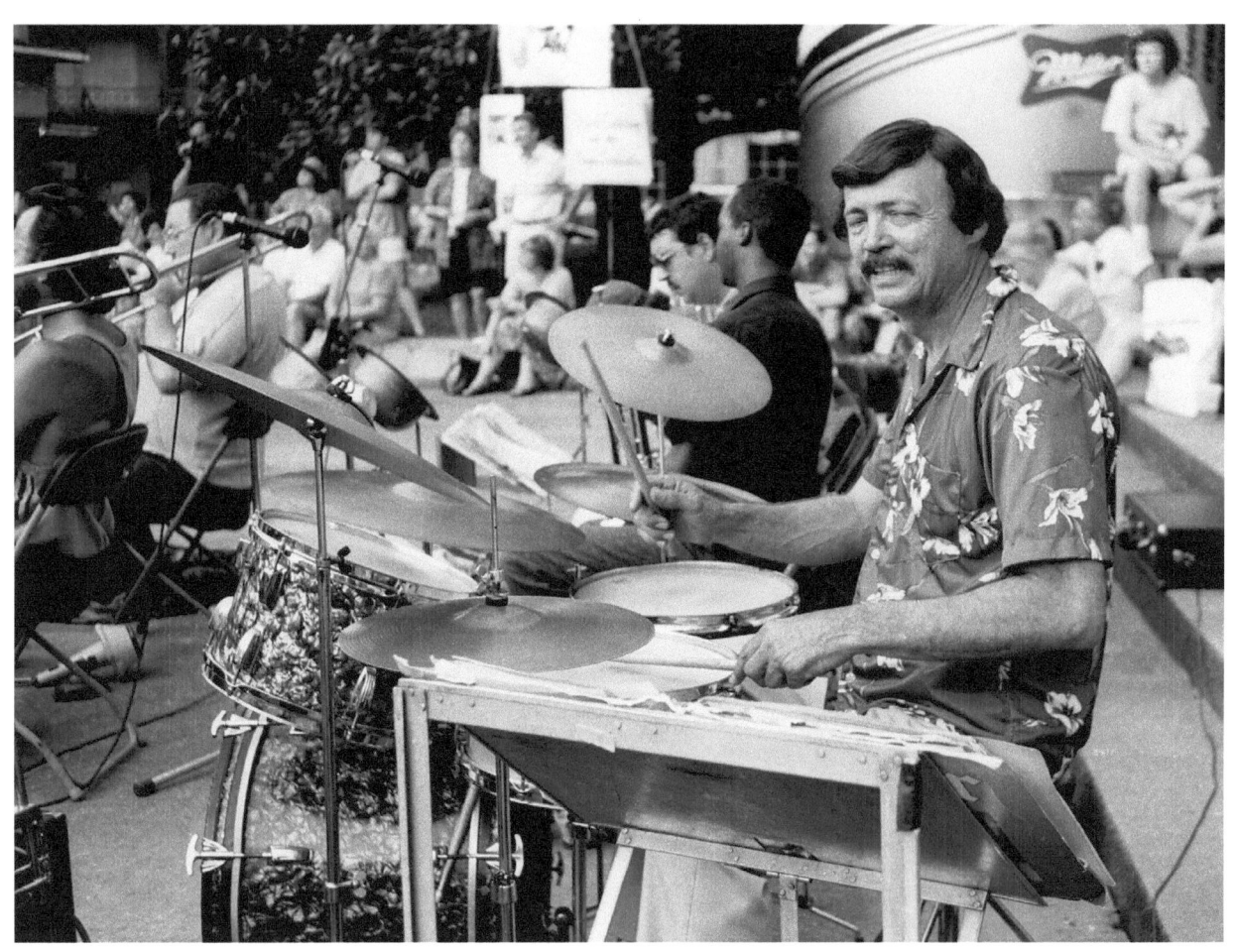

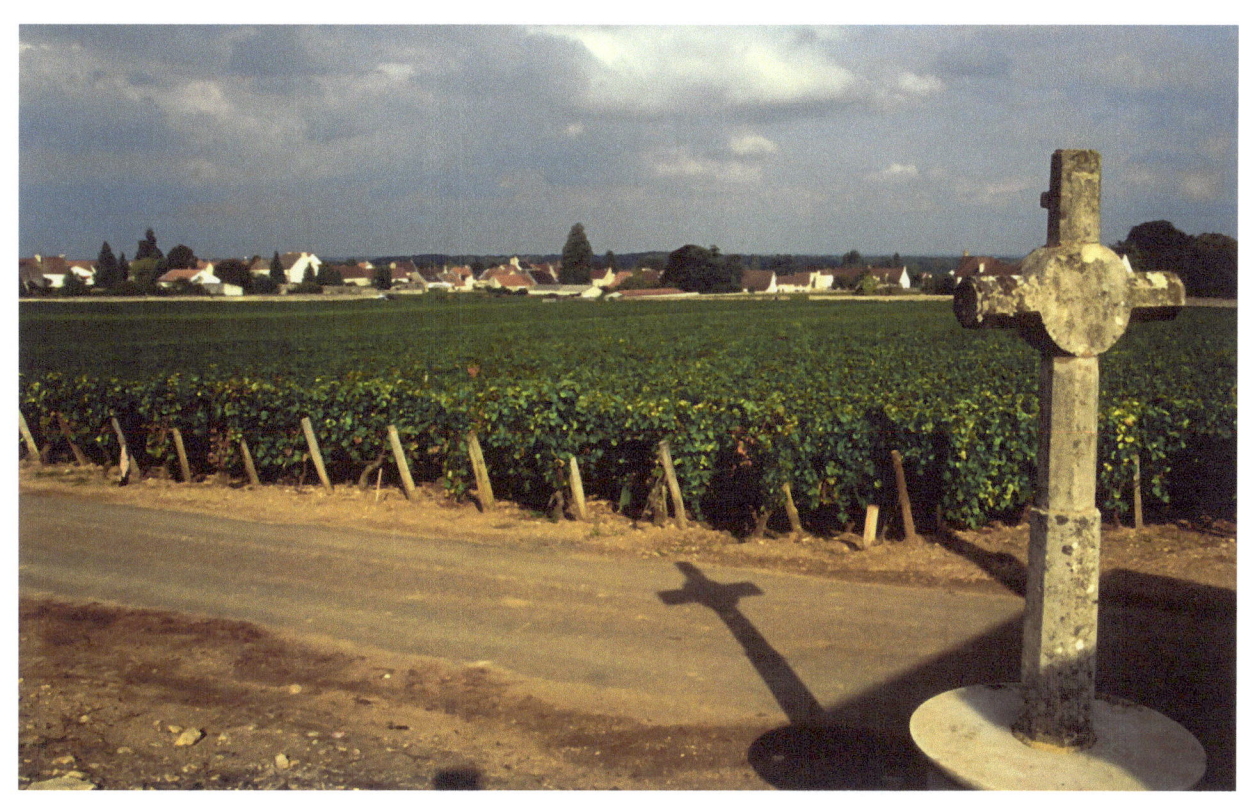

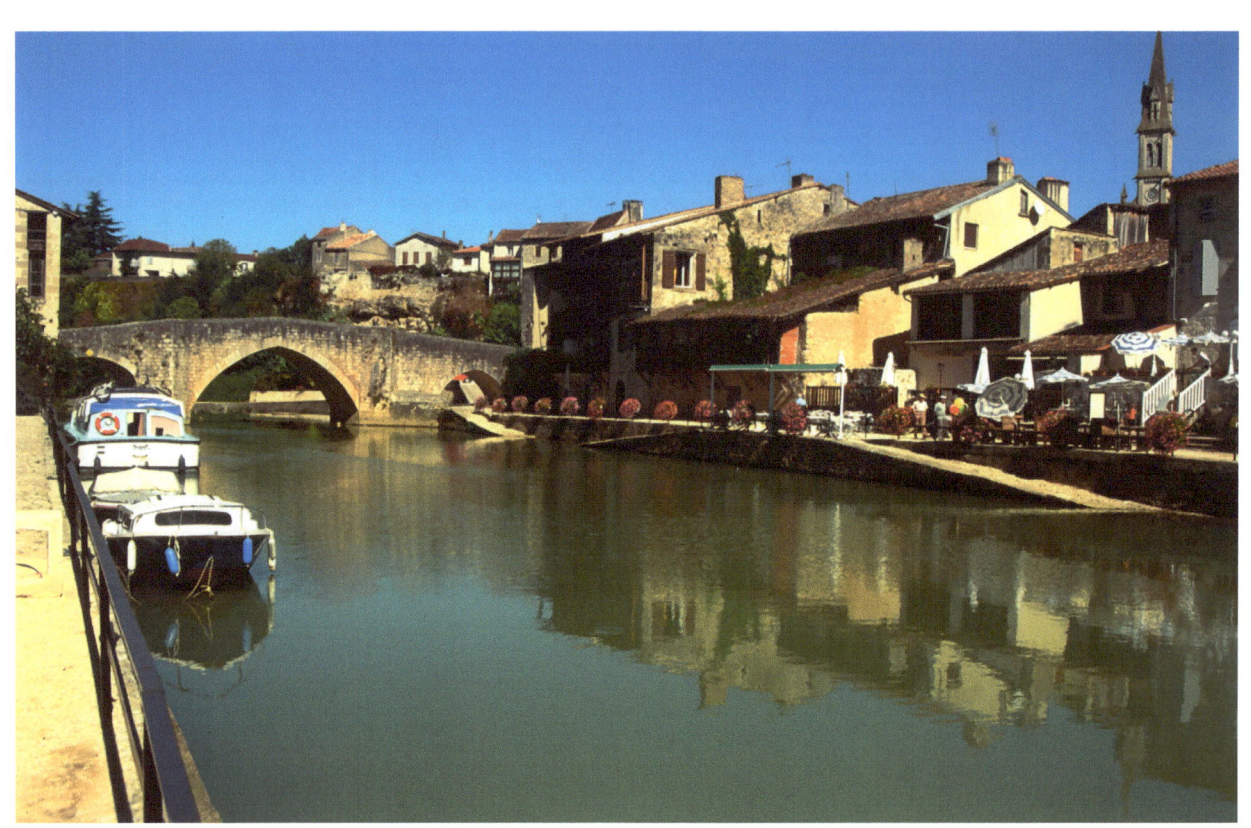

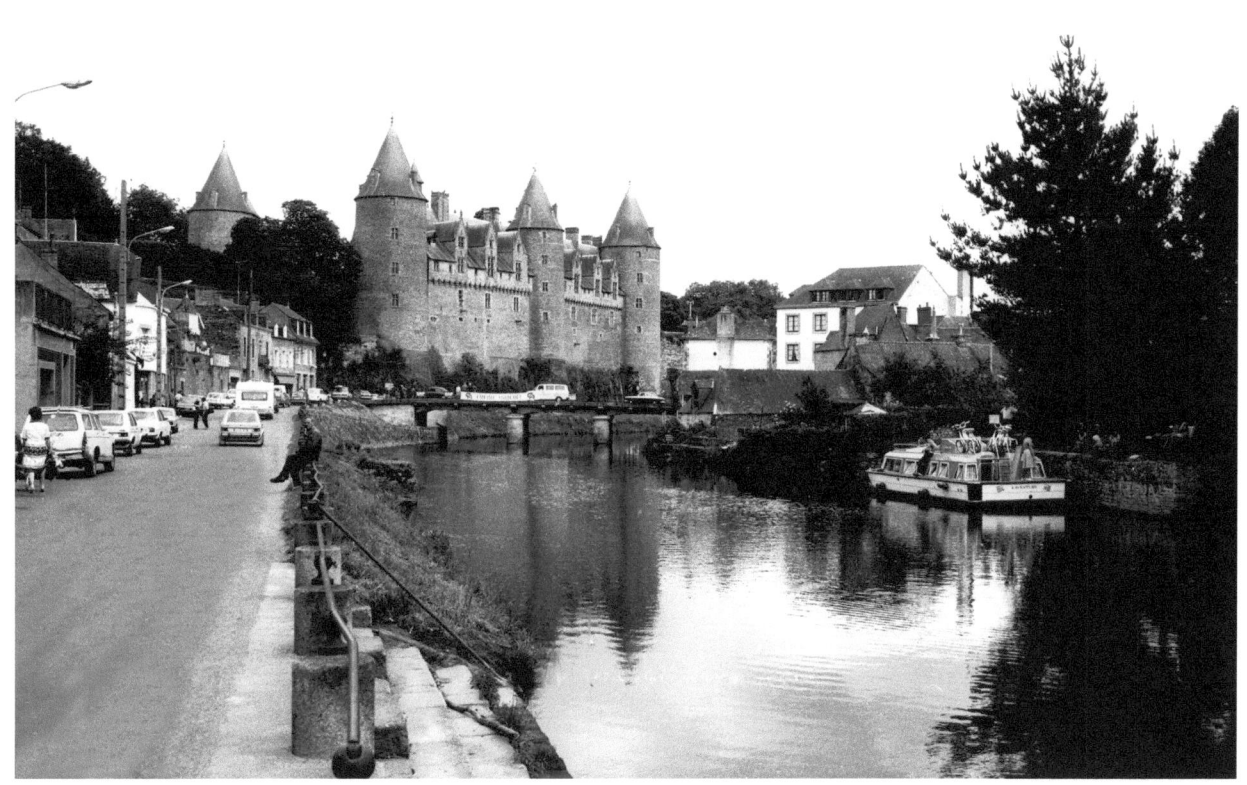

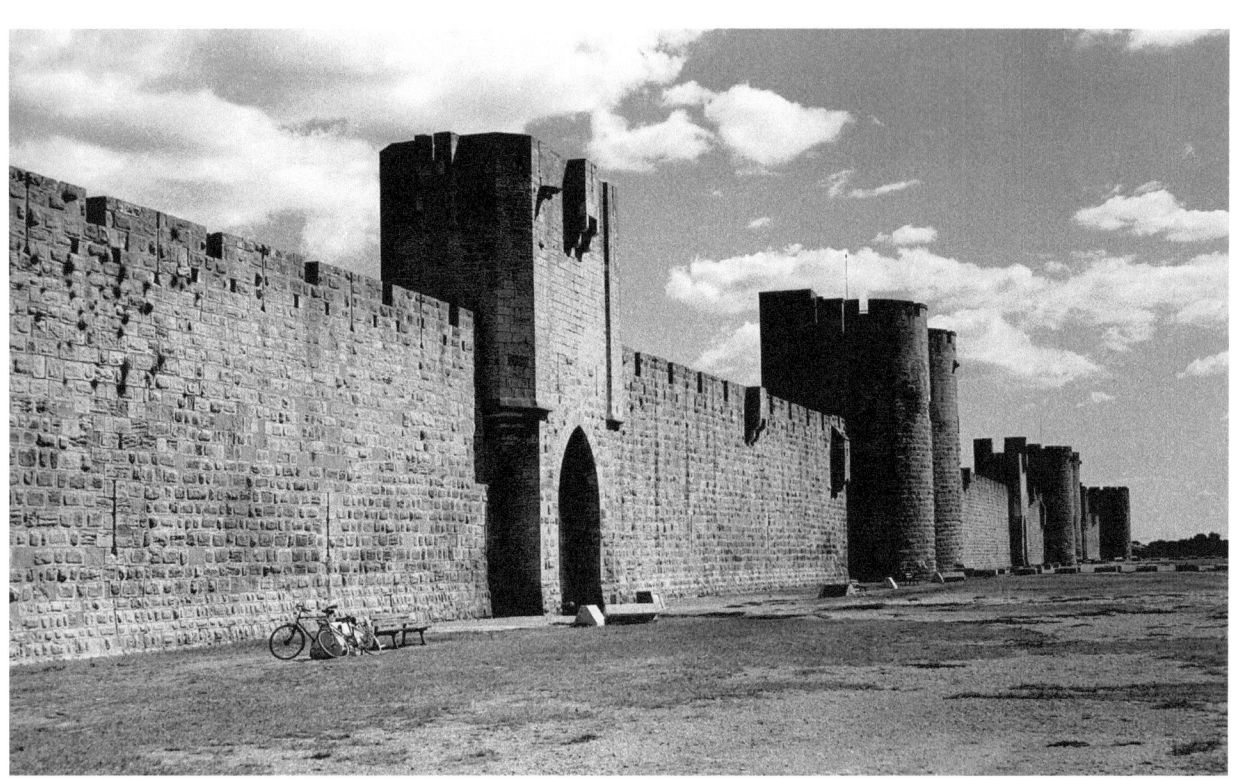

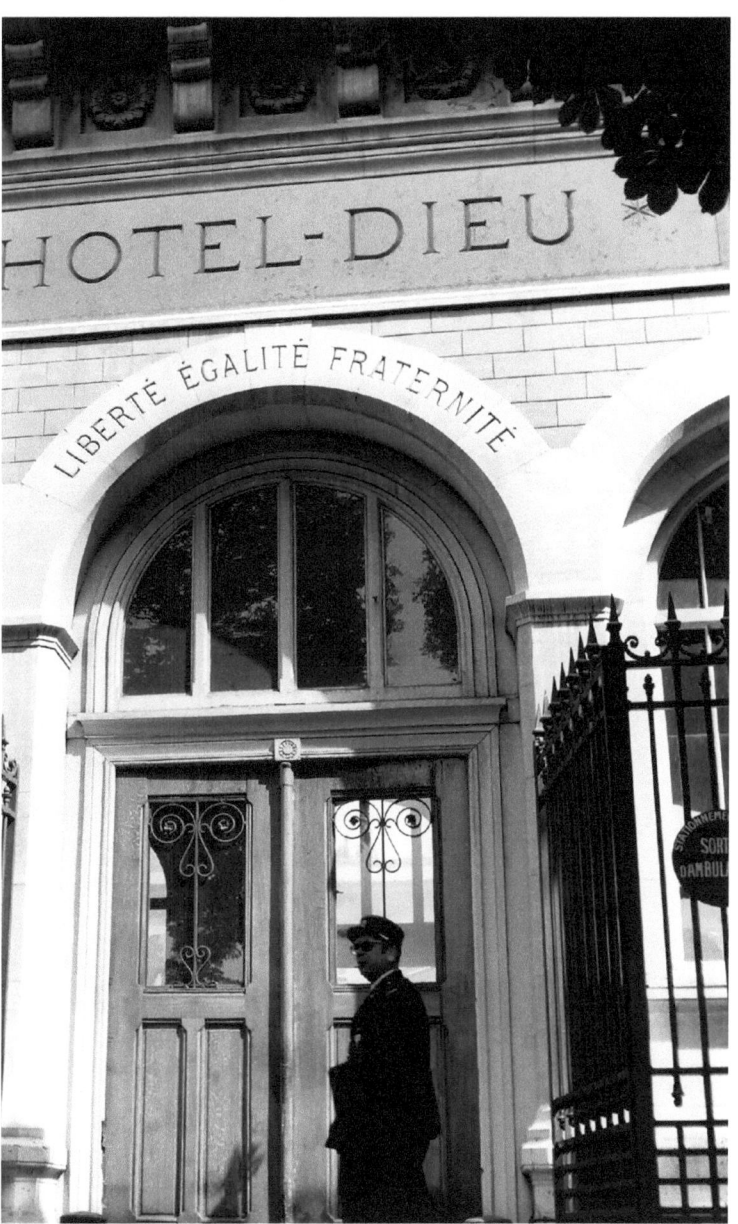

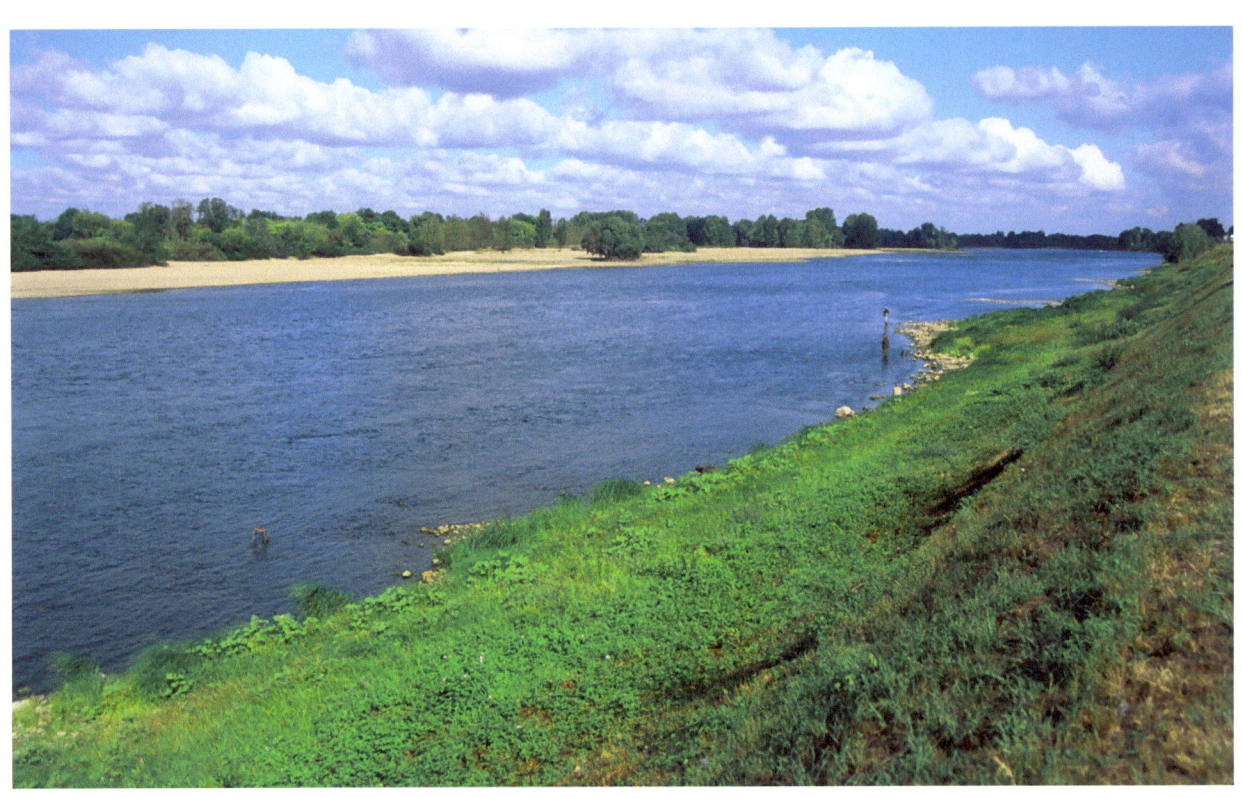

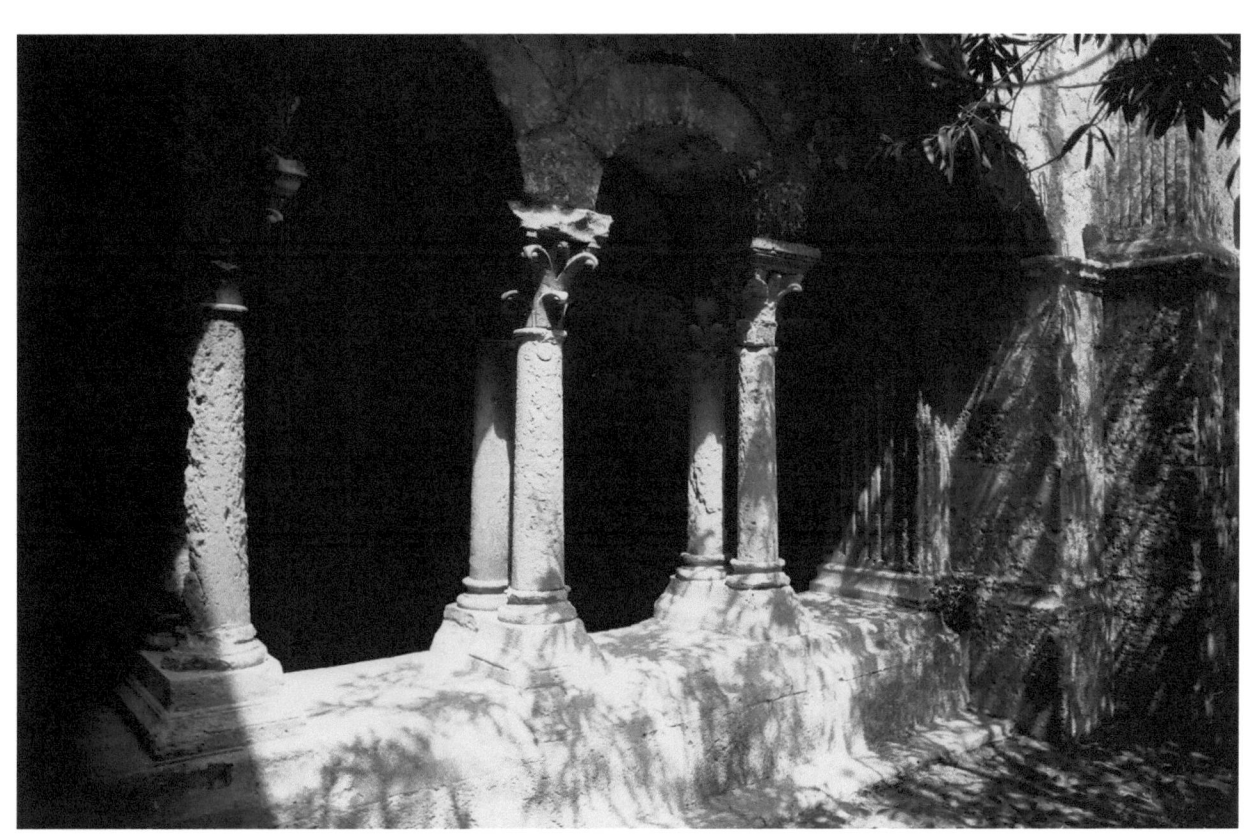

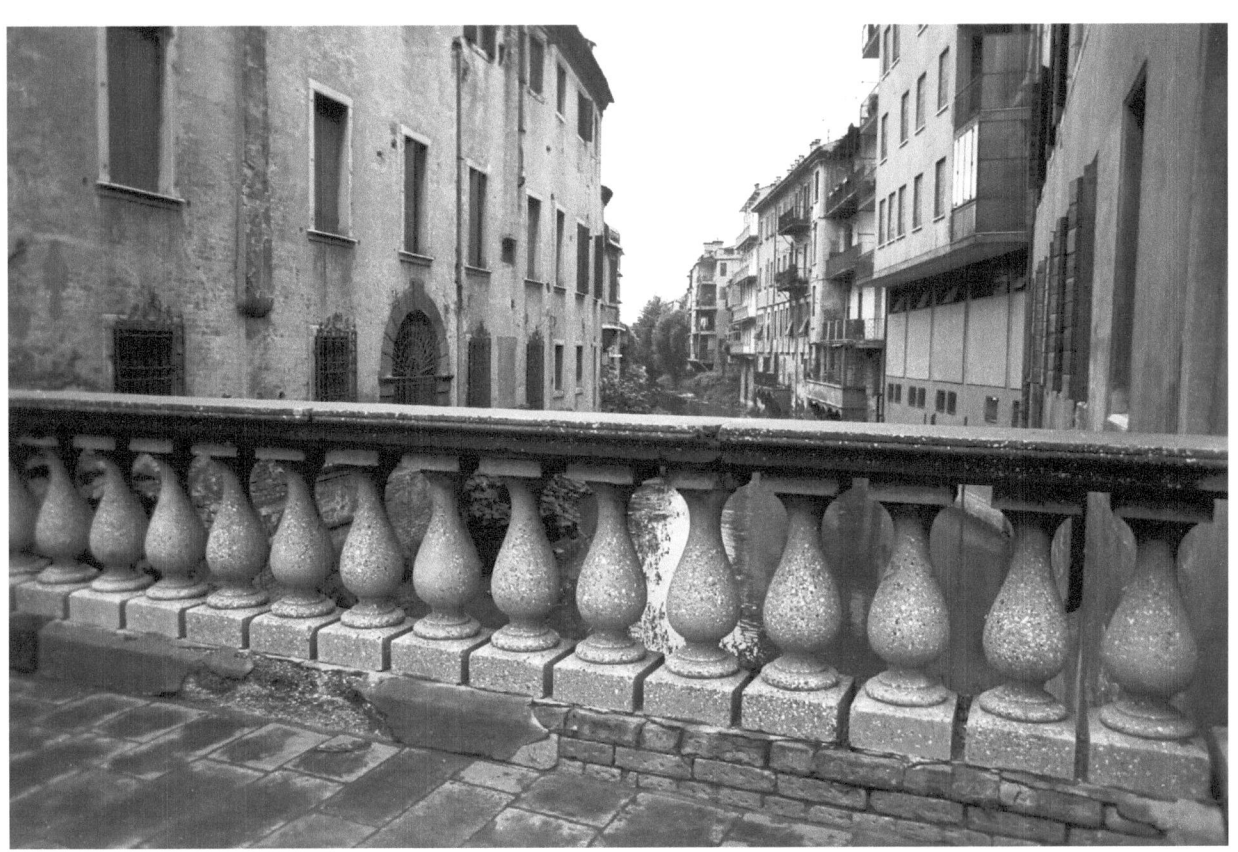

List of photographs

1. Venice, 1974
2. Northern Germany, 1968
3. The Pont Marie is the second-oldest bridge in Paris, in use since 1635
4. Market, Germany, 1967
5. In the historic part of Bremen, Germany
6. A vineyard in Tuscany, Italy
7. Verona, Italy, 1974
8. Venice, grey skies
9. Palermo, Italy, 1967
10. A view of Pompeii with Vesuvius in the background
11. An excursion train in the Ardèche region, France
12. Market day in Darmstadt, Germany. The town's castle (Stadtschloss) can be seen in the background
13. The Nieuwe Kerk, Delft Market Square, Holland, 1968
14. Mount Gerbier de Jonc in the Ardèche region, France. At its foot the river Loire springs to life
15. Near the village of Ste Eulalie the virgin river is gaining strength. In the background Mount Gerbier is barely visible
16. A medieval street in Chinon, France

17. Flea market, Poland, 1996

18. The central railroad station in Milan, Italy (detail)

19. Krakow, Poland

20. Market, Darmstadt, Germany, 1967

21. A famous bargain department store in Toronto, 2006

22. London, 1971

23. London, 1968

24. The windmill of the 19th-century novelist Alphonse Daudet. It stands near the town of Fontvieille in Provence. It is commonly said that his *Lettres de Mon Moulin* originated from the mill, but the work was written in Paris. Today the mill houses a small museum dedicated to the writer

25. The mill as seen from afar

26. Toronto, 1966

27. The market in Delft, Holland, seen from an elevated point

28. Friends meet in a town in Apulia, Italy, 2006

29. Neuharlingersiel, northern Germany, 1968

30. Inside the Abbaye de Fontenay, Burgundy, France

31. La Petite Galette restaurant at the corner of Rue Lepic and Rue Tholozé in Montmartre, Paris. In Jean Renoir's book *Renoir, My Father*, a reference is made to this particular café/restaurant being a haunt of Toulouse-Lautrec.

32. The town of Bruges in Belgium, 1999

33. The railroad viaduct in Barentin, Normandy, France. It carries the Paris–Le Havre railroad and was built in 1846 by the British engineer Joseph Locke, of whom the town erected a statue in his honour

34. Alexanderplatz Station in Berlin, 1991

35. On the rice paddies in South Korea, 1994

36. This young lady did not know that she was being photographed. A real snapshot with a Rolleiflex. Toronto, 1967

37. The Rhône at Avignon, France The view shows the Pont St-Bénézet, the famous bridge, and the Popes' palace behind it

38. The village of Bergheim in the Alsace region of France

39. Newfoundland, Canada, 1975

40. Landscape in the Somme region, northern France. This photo was inspired by the poem 'In Flanders Fields' by John McCrae, a surgeon in the Canadian Army in the Great War. In the background white headstones of a WWI cemetery can be seen

41. The Canadian War Memorial at Vimy Ridge, northern France

42. St Peter's Square, Rome

43. Near Lagos, Algarve, Portugal, 1994

44. A lone windmill stands in a landscape in the south-west of France

45. For generations Parisians have taken their children to the Luxembourg Gardens where they play with their toy sailboats

46. The historic town of Goslar, Germany

47. The bridge south of Arles, Provence, a site which inspired the painter Vincent van Gogh. The beams of the original bridge, which he painted several times, can be seen in the background. The whitewashed building also seems to be the same as in the artist's paintings

48. The so-called White Town of Ostuni, Apulia, Italy

49. The passageway of the synagogue in Cavaillon, France. The synagogue dates from 1772. Situated in the former Jewish quarter of town, it recalls the heritage of a small Jewish community. Located in the old bakery is the Jewish Comtat Venaissin Museum

50. An *Arlésienne*, a woman of Arles, during a festival, 2001

51. Across the Boulevard St Germain in Paris, two famous restaurants face each other: The Deux Magots on the right, and the Brasserie Lipp opposite. Both were haunts of the writers and artists in Paris during the 1920s

52. New Orleans, USA, 1992

53. A vineyard in Burgundy, France

54. The River Baïse in the market town of Nerac in south-west France

55. The River Oust with the castle of Josselin, Brittany, France

56. The walls of Aigues-Mortes on the shores of the Mediterranean. This walled town was founded by the French King Louis IX in the 13th century to give France access to the sea. Marseilles and its port at that time were ruled by the independent Counts of Provence

57. Hôtel-Dieu, Paris

58. The Loire of vineyards and famous châteaux

59. A quiet spot at the abandoned Abbaye de Montmajour, near Arles, France

60. A bridge in Padua, Italy

www.ingramcontent.com/pod-product-compliance
Lightning Source LLC
Chambersburg PA
CBHW041402210526
45162CB00019B/53